THE
ACADEMIC LIBRARY
ADMINISTRATOR'S
FIELD GUIDE

ALA purchases fund advocacy,
awareness, and accreditation programs
for library professionals worldwide.

THE
ACADEMIC LIBRARY
ADMINISTRATOR'S
FIELD GUIDE

BRYCE NELSON

An imprint of the American Library Association

CHICAGO   2014

Bryce Nelson, PhD, was University Librarian at Seattle Pacific University and director of the libraries for the Seattle Public Schools. He is affiliate faculty at the University of Washington's Information School, and Seattle Pacific University's School of Education. He holds degrees from Northwestern University and the University of Washington.

© 2014 by the American Library Association

Printed in the United States of America

18 17 16 15 14   5 4 3 2 1

Extensive effort has gone into ensuring the reliability of the information in this book; however, the publisher makes no warranty, express or implied, with respect to the material contained herein.

ISBNs: 978-0-8389-1223-2 (paper); 978-0-8389-1236-2 (PDF); 978-0-8389-1237-9 (ePub); 978-0-8389-1238-6 (Kindle). For more information on digital formats, visit the ALA Store at alastore.ala.org and select eEditions.

Library of Congress Cataloging-in-Publication Data

Nelson, Bryce Eugene, 1945-
    The academic library administrator's field guide / Bryce Nelson.
      pages   cm
    Includes bibliographical references and index.
    ISBN 978-0-8389-1223-2 (alk. paper)
    1. Academic libraries—Administration—Handbooks, manuals, etc. 2. Academic
libraries—United States—Administration—Handbooks, manuals, etc. I. Title.
    Z675.U5N373 2014
    025.1'977—dc23
                                                                 2014004174

Cover design by Kirstin Krutsch. Images © Shutterstock, Inc. Text design in the Chapparal, Gotham, and Bell Gothic typefaces.

♾ This paper meets the requirements of ANSI/NISO Z39.48-1992 (Permanence of Paper).

Contents

PART I
Being Politically Effective

Acknowledgments

A NUMBER OF PEOPLE READ AND COMMENTED ON VARIOUS iterations of this manuscript, thereby making the resulting book much better than otherwise. I am indebted to all of them for sharing their time, knowledge, and insights: Michael Paulus, Jill McKinstry, Debra Gilchrist, Mark Tucker, Sue Kopp, Dan Bowell, Les Steele, Doug Eriksen, John Bond, Les Foltos, Adam Epp, Dan Johnson, Helene Williams, Tom LaPaze, Dean Erickson, and Clark Johnson. Bonnie Nelson read various versions of this manuscript, and improved the content, writing style, and mechanics. Despite wise counsel and suggestions from these people, the words in this book are mine. I trust that what I wrote is in some way helpful to those who administer academic libraries.

Bryce Nelson
Seattle, WA

Introduction

THIS IS A FIELD GUIDE TO ADMINISTERING AN ACADEMIC library. It consists of:

- topics that matter,
- management advice and research,
- practical applications, and
- citations for further reading.

It is an overview for busy leaders "in the field" who realistically don't have much time to read, think, and talk about their work. Reading in more depth can occur another time, when not "in the field" doing daily administration of a library.

Are there lessons from experience, research, and professional standards which will help in the administration of an academic library? There are, and they are found in a wide variety of books, journal articles, websites, blogs, and conversations with experienced administrators. This volume brings together some of these resources.

The topics are grouped in three sections. The first is about the academic library Director's role in positioning the library as a core part of the institution's educational effort. The next section is about managing staff effectively. When the tasks in these sections are done well, then there is a higher chance of success with the tasks in the third section, providing effective library services.

Advice and research on administration needs to be interpreted and evaluated for their usefulness in a specific library and in its college or university. That takes:

- Judgment ("In what ways is this advice relevant to this place and time?").
- Political awareness ("What is the political cost of a decision?").
- Institutional knowledge ("What do the institution's policies and procedures say about this topic?").

Developing judgment, political awareness, and institutional knowledge takes time and appropriate information. This volume is designed to help with that process.

AUDIENCE

This book is for academic library administrators:

- at any level of experience,
- at any level of administration,
- in a community college, college, or university of any size,
- where research and publication are either valued, or not emphasized, and
- in a public or private college or university.

The key variables which separate academic libraries into significantly different variations are the:

- size of staff,
- relative importance of research, and
- amount of money available to the library.

These variables have significant implications for daily practice. Small-staff libraries are very different places from university research libraries. Nevertheless, this field guide has advice and readings of use to administrators who work in such a wide variety of situations.

This field guide should especially help a new administrator make decisions, decide when to act, and determine what to defer. An academic library administrator is "new" for the first two or three years in that position. Some aspects of the job take several years to learn or influence: for example, the budget cycle. Additionally, there is so much to learn and do in the first year that there is a tendency to become overwhelmed, or overwhelm some of the staff. A new administrator might refer to this field guide on numerous occasions, but need not feel compelled to deal with all topics in it.

After some years of experience, a library administrator may want to rethink some basic assumptions and approaches used in the library. For example:

- Librarian turnover may provide chances to hire for very different roles.
- The campus political context may change with new leadership.
- New technology may alter space, budget, or personnel needs.
- Student learning preferences and faculty assignments could alter the role of the library in learning outcomes.

A veteran administrator might reconsider some aspects of library operation and use this field guide differently than a new administrator.

An administrative field guide is also useful for a library Director's supervisor, both as an overview of the Director's responsibilities and as an aid in guiding conversations. A college or university spends a considerable amount of money on its library. Top administrators want to know how and how well that investment fits into the school's overall teaching, learning, and research agendas. The Director needs to be part of the academic leadership team and demonstrate how the library is part of these agendas. This field guide can help the Director and supervisor talk about how the library is part of the institution's academic life.

This field guide would be useful as an external "voice" in an ongoing conversation between a Director and supervisor. If a Director has a coach/mentor then this field guide would help in that process. A library management class might also use parts or all of it.

DEFINITIONS

Within the community college, college, and university sectors there are multiple terms used to describe similar positions. For consistency and simplicity, I have chosen to standardize terms. The word I use may be different from that used on your campus.

Administrator

The terms administrator, manager, and leader are all used in this book. The term "administrator" refers to those people in a library whose job duties include both managing and leading. They could be the Dean, Associate Dean,

University Librarian, Director, Associate Director, or department head. When any administrator acts as a manager, the person is accountable for the conditions under which others work and the quality of their work. When an administrator provides leadership, that person asks if a task, service, or person is necessary, leads an evaluation, and then uses his or her influence to make a change.

Director

The administrator who leads an academic library might have the title of Dean, University Librarian, Director, or even another term. I use the term "Director" to cover any title that refers to the administrator who leads an academic library, including those in small-staff libraries who simultaneously do librarian and administrative work.

Provost

The person the Director reports to is commonly the top administrator with responsibility for academic affairs, or someone close to that level. The title of that person might be Provost, Vice President, Dean, or some variation. I use the term "Provost" to refer to the person who is the supervisor of the library Director.

Academic Library

I use the term "academic library" to refer to a library or library system in an institution of higher education. That institution of any size could be a community college, college, or university, public or private. The library consists of a physical building (or buildings) and a virtual presence organized through its website.

Library Staff

The term "library staff" refers to all who work in a library who are not administrators. Some will be professional librarians. Librarians often have faculty status. Other staff perform non-librarian roles and may be unionized. I use the term "library staff" to refer to all except administrators and student employees.

ORGANIZATION OF THIS FIELD GUIDE

This book is organized into thirty topical chapters. The chapters need not be read sequentially, nor does the book need to be read cover to cover. Rather, as a field guide, an individual chapter is best read when there is a need for information on that topic.

The chapters are grouped into three sections, representing three areas within which academic library administrators have the responsibility for making decisions. The premise is sequential. First, the Director must be politically effective among other campus administrators. Second, the Director (and other library administrators) must be competent managers of library staff. If successful in those two areas, then the library administrators are more likely to manage the operational side of the library at an effective level.

PART I
BEING POLITICALLY EFFECTIVE

The operation of an academic library is nested within the overall administration of the college or university. The supervisor of the library Director is usually an academic leader (e.g., Provost) who has influence over the library in terms of budget, hiring, space, and strategic direction. The library Director is one of many other administrators (e.g., Deans and Vice Presidents) who compete for money, space, personnel, and status for the colleges, schools, or departments they lead. The Provost tries to balance competing needs, all within the institution's goals and budget. The library Director must understand the organizational chart and how decisions are made, resources allocated, and services evaluated. The Director must learn to be a politically effective advocate for the library. That requires being a member of the campus leadership team. Thinking and acting politically mean understanding formal and informal influence relative to other administrators and units of the institution, making and using personal connections, and factoring in the longer-term consequences of decisions.

PART II
MANAGING AND LEADING STAFF

Managing and leading staff is the hardest part of a library administrator's job. It can cause the most anxiety, but also provide considerable satisfaction during those times when things go well. The variables that make up the culture and effectiveness of a staff are always moving and aren't always self-evident. A good administrator sets the conditions for hiring, professional development, evaluation, and decision-making. Administrators need to know the recent work history of staff, the history of the library within the institution, and stay informed about the work all library staff are doing. How a library Director begins and ends a tenure has much to do with the level of success for that person, and for the library.

PART III
SUPERVISING OPERATIONS

Skillful library administrators manage the routine operations of a library so well that few people even notice. Uneventful daily operation is the goal. This occurs when:

- procedures are clear,
- budget is adequate to provide content and services close to what users want, and
- building and technical infrastructure work as they were designed.

However, when the quality is below expectations, or some operation breaks down (and there is no "Plan B" ready to go), then assertive complaints will likely be aimed at the Director.

ORGANIZATION WITHIN EACH CHAPTER

The format of this field guide consists of thirty chapters, each discussing a topic that is part of an administrator's responsibilities. Each of the chapters is divided into four sections. The sections are organized in descending order, from the conceptual to the application. Each topic begins with a conceptual Assertion. Following, the Commentary paragraphs provide perspective and general advice. The Application section has examples of "good practices." The Reading section contains citations to research and advice.

Assertion

Each chapter is introduced with an Assertion, which is a conceptual statement about the topic from the administrator's perspective. Is this valid for a library in the context of its educational institution? The Assertion drives the content in the Commentary, Application, and Reading sections. Hence, the validity of the Assertion may well influence decision making on that topic.

Commentary

The Commentary section gives observations about the conceptual Assertion statement. These paragraphs are reminders of what to consider when thinking about this topic. If these Commentary paragraphs are not useful for a specific context, then they may serve the purpose of helping an administrator reflect more accurately on what is useful for the institution.

Application

The Application section gives examples of "good practices." The administrator needs to evaluate which of these may be useful in this library, institution, and time. All of these examples may not be relevant. Instead, they may serve as reminders of what to pay attention to, and what to alter so that it works in a specific context.

Reading

The Reading section provides references to books, articles, websites, and blogs that may be useful for further reading on the chapter's topic. Grouped first are references with links to standards and guidelines. Following are citations to advice and research-based material. Depending on the size and type of academic library, some of the readings cited may be less about administration and more about that topic, and hence too specific for some readers. In a library with a larger staff, someone else will know specific material about that topic, and the Director will only need to know at a conceptual level. Or, in a small-staff library, the Director may need more of a working knowledge of many topics in order to make decisions, even collaborative decisions. The works cited are mostly from an administrative perspective, but there are also works cited from a librarian's perspective that get fairly specific.

SUMMARY

This is a field guide for those who administer academic libraries. It is designed to give such people a reminder about what topics are important and how to think about those topics, and provide readers with some examples of good practices, as well as citations to advice and research. The intent is to help an administrator make and implement better decisions than without this guidance.

PART I
Being Politically Effective

An academic library Director must be part of the campus administrative team, and be politically effective on behalf of the library. This is where the Director's work starts. If the Director is not politically effective, then the chances of competently managing and leading staff (Part II) and operations (Part III) are compromised.

1
Rationale

Mission, Goals, and Strategic Plan

ASSERTION

The academic library Director establishes a process that keeps the library's mission, goals, and strategic plan aligned with the college or university's educational program.

COMMENTARY

Mission Statement

A successful academic library program begins with a succinct mission statement that is closely aligned with the academic part of the college or university's mission statement. The library statement might use some of the institution's same words. The statement needs to say that the library exists because it is a necessary, basic, core, or fundamental part of the institution's educational mission. It does not need to say much more. A useful mission statement is short, and has a few words or phrases which most people can remember.

A library mission statement which is not closely derived from the educational emphasis in the institution's mission statement, or which wanders with additional purposes, invites a perception that the library is supplemental rather than a core part of the school's academic purposes. Top administrators spent time writing and vetting the institution's mission statement, and these words influence decisions ranging from budget and facilities to accreditation. If the President, Provost, and Vice Presidents cannot see their educational words reflected in the library's mission statement, then it is easier for them to perceive the library as supplemental and take the library for granted. When the library's mission statement contains words that are the same as the institution's words about its educational mission, then the library has a better chance of being a necessary part of the institution's teaching, learning, and research agendas.

Library Goals

Just as the library mission statement must be derived from the college or university's mission statement, the library goals must also be derived from the institution's academic goals. Top administrators need to see alignment between the library and the institutional academic goals. Using some of the same words is helpful.

Strategic Plan

A library strategic plan is derived from its mission statement and goals, which is another reason why those words matter. A strategic plan needs to be renewed every several years, on a schedule. The strategic plan defines the priorities of library staff, and shows campus administrators (and accreditors) how and when the library is implementing parts of the institutional strategic plan.

It is easy for the terms in a library strategic plan to be too library-centric. The library Director and staff need to write a plan for the library that references how teaching, learning, research, and funding are done (and might be changing) in the institution. Ideally the financial resources follow the right vision and its derived plan. Library administrators need to be part of the campus "brain trust," to help push the institution beyond where it has been educationally. Library staff and administrators have a campus-wide view of teaching, learning, and research and have valuable insights to share. One purpose of an effective library strategic plan is to inform the campus community about the roles the library does and can play, timelines, and the cost and benefits of those emerging roles.

APPLICATION

Writing the Mission Statement

Writing the mission statement is a process shared by as many library staff as possible. It is wise to set aside time to work on this in a staff retreat, such as prior to the start of the academic year. Provide readings on what a mission statement should be, and that also show examples of mission statements well-aligned between an institution and its library. Invite a facilitator to lead the staff through the process of writing a mission statement (and goals and a strategic plan). Ask an academic administrator to talk to the staff about the current institutional mission statement and academic goals.

One way to start the process of writing a library mission statement is to look at the words of the college or university mission statement. Identify how many of these words can be used to answer the question of why this institution has a library program. Do the same with the statements for accreditation (e.g., core themes, goals, or standards) and use those words where feasible. Start with what is already written, identify key words and phrases, and try to incorporate those into a very short library mission statement.

Writing the Goal Statements

Writing goals is a process best combined with writing a mission statement and strategic plan. Inviting an academic administrator to talk with the staff about the institution's academic direction will improve the library goals. It also "says" to the administrator that the library staff are trying to align its resources and work with the academic direction of the institution. Look at the college or university goals, follow that format, and use the same words and phrases as much as possible. Make a chart with columns listing the institutional and library goals. Make it obvious that library efforts align with the institution's academic intent.

Writing the Strategic Plan

Writing the strategic plan should also be part of a staff effort to write the mission statement and goals. This is the document that outlines what library staff and administrators agree to do during the several years of this strategic plan. Administrators are responsible for the use of staff time, and the plan is that guide. Both administrators and staff should understand that things change, and that realistically some items in the plan will need to be modified or dropped during the plan's timeframe.

Using Graphics

A good mission statement consists of one or two simple sentences. Out of those words there might be three or four words that capture the essence of the statement, and that people might actually remember and use. A few words in a graphic representation can be a useful shorthand version of a mission statement.

Displaying the Mission Statement

Print, frame, and display multiple copies of the library mission statement and put these in predictable as well as surprising places around the library. This is especially useful if the mission statement can be summarized in a few words, and portrayed graphically in a way that people can remember. A framed graphic can go on walls in library work areas and in a few public areas. Advertise these words on the library website, the signature line of library staff on e-mails, on coffee cups for the library staff, or on advertising you give away (e.g., pencils or plastic book bags). By using several key words from your mission statement, you are saying over and over that this library is a foundational (not supplemental) part of what this institution does, and that the campus community should pay attention.

Invoking the Unofficial Mission Phrase

There is the written, vetted, published library mission statement, and then there is the unofficial "mission phrase" in the Director's head. This is the driving phrase that gives urgency to an administrator's work, but probably should be kept private. Think of a library that has better indicators, but which your library may be able to equal or surpass. With some self-deprecating humor, tell yourself that the "real" mission statement is "Beat [name of school]." By aspiring to surpass another library on some pre-determined benchmarks, you have another way to chart your yearly progress. Invoking the name of an aspirational library can keep you focused on a few indicators.

READING

STANDARDS AND GUIDELINES

American Association of Community Colleges. "AACC Position Statement on Library and Learning Resource Center Programs." Washington, D.C.: American Association of Community Colleges, 2003. www.aacc.nche.edu/About/Positions/Pages/ps01062003.aspx.

Association of College and Research Libraries. "Guidelines for University Library Services to Undergraduate Students." Chicago: American Library Association, 2005, 2013. www.ala.org/acrl/standards/ulsundergraduate.

Association of College and Research Libraries. "The Role of the Community College Library in the Academy." Chicago: American Library Association. www.ala.org/acrl/issues/roleofcommcollege.

Association of College and Research Libraries. "Standards for Libraries in Higher Education." Chicago: American Library Association, 2011. www.ala.org/acrl/standards/standardslibraries.

ADVICE AND RESEARCH

Alire, Camila A., and G. Edward Evans. *Academic Librarianship*. New York: Neal-Schuman Publishers, Inc., 2010.

Berstler, Andrea D. "Running the Library As a Business." In *The Entrepreneurial Librarian: Essays on the Infusion of Private-Business Dynamism into the Professional Service*, edited by Mary Krautter, Mary Beth Lock, and Mary G. Scanlon. Jefferson, NC: McFarland & Company, Inc., 2012.

Birdsall, Douglas G. "Strategic Planning in Academic Libraries: A Political Perspective." In *Restructuring Academic Libraries: Organizational Development in the Wake of Technological Change, Publications in Librarianship No. 49*. Chicago: American Library Association, n.d. www.ala.org/acrl/publications/booksanddigitalresources/booksmonographs/pil/pil49/pil49restructuring.

Cottrell, Janet R. "What Are We Doing Here, Anyway? Tying Academic Library Goals to Institutional Mission." *College & Research Libraries News* 72 no. 9 (2011): 516–520. http://crln.acrl.org/content/72/9/516.full.

Dowell, David R., and Gerard B. McCabe, editors. *It's All About Student Learning. Managing Community and Other College Libraries in the 21st Century*. Westport, CT: Libraries Unlimited, 2006.

Dubicki, Eleonora, compiler and editor. *Strategic Planning in College Libraries*. CLIP Note #43. Chicago: Association of College and Research Libraries, 2011.

Estabrook, Leigh S. "What Chief Academic Officers Want from Their Libraries: Findings from Interviews with Provosts and Chief Academic Officers." Chicago: Association of College and Research Libraries, 2007. www.ala.org/acrl/sites/ala.org.acrl/files/content/publications/whitepapers/Finalreport-ACRLCAOs.pdf.

Long, Matthew P., and Roger C. Schonfeld. "Ithaka S+R Library Survey 2010: Insights from U.S. Academic Library Directors," 2011. www.sr.ithaka.org/research-publications/library-survey-2010.

Matthews, Joseph R. *Library Assessment in Higher Education*. Westport, CT: Libraries Unlimited, 2007.

"Value of Academic and Research Libraries." Chicago: Association of College and Research Libraries. www.ala.org/acrl/issues/value and www.acrl.ala.org/value.

2
Perceptions

Library Components Are Basic to Education

ASSERTION

The academic library Director leads in ways that result in the library's component parts (staff, services, space, website, online resources, and physical collections) being fundamentally necessary and basic parts of the educational process.

COMMENTARY

Educational Role

The academic library Director needs to do what is possible to shape the reality and perception held by students, faculty, and administrators that the library is a necessary and basic part of education on this campus. The library's component parts (staff, services, space, website, online resources, and physical collections) are necessary for teaching, learning, discovery, and research. These terms define the educational roles of an academic library, with "research" being the variable, depending on the type of institution. The relative importance of research will in turn drive library staffing, collections, and space.

Teaching. Librarians have a role in teaching and curricular design. This may include "information literacy," critical thinking skills, and the process of researching in the disciplines. Especially when librarians work closely with departmental faculty, then they are instructors who also work on curriculum, pedagogy, and (sometimes) student assessment. In some places, librarians teach courses on the use of the library in inquiry-based learning, especially to first-year students. Librarians teach when they consult with students and faculty on research projects, or teach about the use of technology, software, and applications. Library instructional roles also include how the website is organized and the building space is arranged, what services are offered, and training is provided to the student workers.

Learning. The library's role in student learning is to provide content, spaces, network access, computing equipment, software, a website, and staff assistance. All of these parts are intentionally designed to result in successful student learning outcomes. The institution may have a set of learning outcomes for undergraduate students, and the educational role of the library should be evident when viewing those outcomes.

Discovery. Faculty and students discover desired content through the library's systems software, its collections, and librarian knowledge of how to navigate in order to find what is desired.

Research. The library's role in research is to provide (or provide access to) books, peer-reviewed journals, archival materials, and other scholarly literature for academic research on a topic. Librarians may also help during and after research with issues around publication.

It is easy for students and faculty to take an academic library for granted, especially a good academic library. It is also easy for some in the campus community to see the library as a "support" service, rather like the bookstore, Information Technology, or food service. If the library is perceived as a "support service" (rather than as a basic part of the educational process), then the library will slowly move to the political and budgetary margins of the institution.

A basic role for the Director is to lead, encourage, and support the librarians as educators, integrated into the academic life of the institution. How well the librarians directly contribute to the aspects of academic life valued in that institution (teaching, learning, discovery, and research) is the basis against which the library is judged, and its political standing determined. The default approach of the Director and librarians should be to ask themselves in what ways they are part of the successful educational experience of students.

Perceptions from Other Administrators

The budget and status of the library program are influenced by images of the library held by Deans and other top administrators. These images come from many sources:

- experiences with libraries at other schools,
- past and current use of any library by these administrators,
- current data about the use and impact of this library,
- experiences with past Directors,
- observations of the current Director, and
- past history of library personnel issues.

Campus administrators need to see and hear current images of the educational contributions of the library. The Director needs to be attuned to that, be ahistorical, and provide new images to replace lingering old ones.

Perceptions from Faculty and Students

The Director and the librarians need to work continuously to show students how this library is an essential part of their learning. Many students do not know much about the library, or initially care about the library. Even if students come to college or university with a good high school library experience, an academic library is qualitatively different from what they previously experienced. Librarians especially need to teach about the value of the library to first-year students, upper-division students with majors, and graduate students writing theses and dissertations.

Faculty have a wide variety of experiences and expectations about a library. Librarians need to make personal contacts with faculty and demonstrate the many ways in which they can work with instructors in their teaching and research. The approach of the library Director and librarians needs to be active, not passive. A liaison model in which almost all of the librarians have departmental responsibilities is a very effective way to make and sustain contacts with faculty, and influence perceptions.

Director's Rank and Privileges

Because the library plays an educational role, then the library Director is better served by having faculty rank and privileges. What "faculty rank and privileges" means is already defined and implemented by each institution's governing structure. It is desirable that the library Director has rank and privileges similar to those of the academic Deans (e.g., rank, promotion, tenure).

The issue of rank and promotion for a library Director often involves the expectation for scholarly research and publication. Some institutions grant rank, but do not expect the Director to do research and publish. Managing a library well is an all-consuming job. There isn't much time for research and writing at the level that would result in publication. If the institutional expectation is that a Director will publish, then the Director needs a leave, sabbatical, or a temporary move to part-time status.

Librarian Rank and Privileges

Because the library plays an educational role, the librarians should have faculty status. The Director needs to advocate for librarians to have faculty rank and privileges and be evaluated as faculty.

The models for faculty status vary widely among institutions. The Director needs to interpret what faculty status, rank, and privileges mean in practice in the institution. The Director must first build consensus among the librarians regarding the nature of the librarian's work, how to describe that work to classroom faculty, and the criteria used to evaluate the quality of the librarian's work. The important variable is whether or not librarians are expected to do research and publish, or be evaluated on the basis of competence in librarianship without publication. That usually means the quality of their teaching, discipline knowledge, advising of students, and service in governance activities.

The Director also needs to work with the faculty evaluation committee to interpret the criteria for instructional faculty so that the librarians can be evaluated on criteria appropriate for them. If it isn't clear to members of a faculty evaluation committee why librarians are faculty, and how to distinguish levels of competence in librarianship, then the process of evaluating faculty librarians for promotion in rank can be baffling.

APPLICATION

Annual Reports

The academic library Director should write an Annual Report at the end of each fiscal year, organized around the themes of the institution's accreditation report, and post a link to the current and previous annual reports on the library website. The Director needs to find ways to convey to the campus community some stories and statistics from the Annual Report that illustrate how the library contributes to the institution's educational efforts. Good news about the library needs to be shared. A few pieces of positive news at the start of the school year can be e-mailed to faculty and administrators (and maybe to the students), with a link to an executive summary of the Annual

Report. Sometimes campus communication staff are open to putting library success stories in the campus publications, e-newsletters, websites, blogs, and advertisements.

Images

The Director needs to "sell" the future vision of the library by using photographs, charts, and graphs that show how the library is an essential component of the educational process. Images convey the current definition of "library." In e-mails to faculty and students, it is wise to use relatively fewer words and instead use images designed to make an impression. As examples:

- Chart the use of e-resources.
- Chart the amount of collaborative teaching done by librarians.
- Show data on information literacy outcomes.
- Show photographs of "active learning" teaching occurring in desirable library spaces, with students using laptops and tablets.
- Show photographs of studio or workshop spaces in the library where students use collaborative technology to work on projects.
- Show photographs of student art or class projects on display in the library.

By being very intentional, it is possible to shape an image of the library by using photographs, charts, and graphs that administrators, faculty, and students will notice and remember. Show them current images about the library's educational roles.

Tagline

Create a tagline for the library that reminds the campus community of specific library roles with students and faculty in teaching, learning, research, and the dissemination of that knowledge. Put that tagline everywhere, such as on the website, on staff e-mail signature lines, on walls in the library, and on whatever you give away as advertising. For example, many libraries supply free pencils, bookmarks, or plastic bags for books. Whatever you give away, view it as advertising for the library, and have printed on it the library URL and tagline.

Departmental Reviews

Academic departments are normally reviewed on a rotating schedule by a faculty oversight committee. The curriculum, faculty, budget, and equipment are all examined. These departmental reviews are good opportunities to examine the role of the library for that department. It is better to have the performance of the library for that department included on the checklist, rather than be overlooked.

Tour

When there is a new President, Provost, Vice President or Dean, at some point in that person's first year invite him or her to the library for a walking tour. Use this time to talk about the vision of where the library is headed, and show the projects already under way that are part of the educational mission. The Director gets one chance to do this. Shape the tour and message to highlight the good things occurring. Don't talk about needs and wants. Top administrators rarely enter the library, and rarely receive a tour that highlights how the library fits directly into teaching, learning, and research. They probably expect a request for a budget increase. There will be other times to talk about money.

"Seeing" the Library

The library needs to be "seen" in a variety of institutional planning documents, or else the library will drift farther away from being a core part of the institution's educational tasks. It is desirable if the word "library" is written in documents at the level of the institution's goals, objectives, or core values. It is very desirable if the library is mentioned in a strategic plan, which guides changes (and budget) in an institution. The perspective of an academic library Director needs to be represented at the tables where such documents are written. The library is part of the educational equation, but for a variety of reasons can be overlooked. Hence, the library Director must be aware of each committee preparing a document that describes the institution's teaching, learning, and research efforts. The Director needs to use some political influence early in the process to make sure that a committee "sees" the role of the library and writes it into a document.

READING

STANDARDS AND GUIDELINES

Association of College and Research Libraries. "A Guideline for the Appointment, Promotion and Tenure of Academic Librarians." Chicago: Association of College and Research Libraries, 2010. www.ala.org/acrl/standards/promotiontenure.

Association of College and Research Libraries. "Guidelines for Academic Librarians Without Faculty Status." Chicago: Association of College and Research Libraries, 2011. www.ala.org/acrl/standards/guidelinesacademic.

Association of College and Research Libraries. "Guidelines for University Library Services to Undergraduate Students." Chicago: American Library Association, 2005, 2013. www.ala.org/acrl/standards/ulsundergraduate.

Association of College and Research Libraries. "Joint Statement on Faculty Status of College and University Librarians." Chicago: Association of College and Research Libraries, Association of American Colleges, and the American Association of University Professors, 2012. www.ala.org/acrl/standards/jointstatementfaculty.

Association of College and Research Libraries. "Standards for Faculty Status for Academic Librarians." Chicago: Association of College and Research Libraries, 2011. www.ala.org/acrl/standards/standardsfaculty.

Association of College and Research Libraries. "Standards for Libraries in Higher Education." Chicago: American Library Association, 2011. www.ala.org/acrl/standards/standardslibraries.

ADVICE AND RESEARCH

Alire, Camila A., and G. Edward Evans. *Academic Librarianship*. New York: Neal-Schuman Publishers, Inc., 2010.

Applegate, Rachel. *Managing the Small College Library*. Santa Barbara, CA: Libraries Unlimited, 2010.

Dowell, David R., and Gerard B. McCabe, eds. *It's All About Student Learning. Managing Community and Other College Libraries in the 21st Century*. Westport, CT: Libraries Unlimited, 2006.

Long, Matthew P., and Roger C. Schonfeld. "Ithaka S+R Library Survey 2010: Insights from U.S. Academic Library Directors," 2011. www.sr.ithaka.org/research-publications/library-survey-2010.

Matthews, Joseph R. *Library Assessment in Higher Education*. Westport, CT: Libraries Unlimited, 2007.

3
Political Influence

Roles of an Effective Leader

ASSERTION

The academic library Director is part of the campus leadership team and, for the political well-being of the library, needs to be an effective part of this leadership team.

COMMENTARY

Being Political

The position of the academic library Director is very political, and the Director needs to understand that and then think and act politically. That means always trying to understand:

- the institutional context within which the library operates,
- who influences which decisions,
- who makes which decisions,
- the amount of political capital held by the library, and
- the longer-term consequences of actions.

There are turning points which can set a library on a positive or negative trajectory. While the quality of the library cannot be masked by the Director's political skill, nevertheless, where there is a quality library program (or an improving library program), then a Director (or series of Directors) has effectively cultivated relationships of influence and managed without serious mistakes.

Being an Administrator

Holding an administrative position means that a librarian has crossed a line from being faculty or staff, and has now become part of the campus leadership team and its culture. On the administrative side of that line are responsibilities, allegiances, social connections, and information that are not present on the librarian side. That requires learning an "administrative" way of thinking and acting in that part of one's work life. The Director is the "face" of the library among campus administrators, and so must be aware of that role in all situations. There will be access to a different kind of information than before. The administrator must learn what to write and say to whom (and when), and what to keep confidential. The administrator's relationships with members of the faculty and staff will change. The Director especially will spend time with a new set of work and social groups.

In libraries with a small staff, where the Director does both administrative and librarian work, the Director crosses the line multiple times each day between being a librarian and a campus administrator. Not only does the Director need to know what it means when switching roles, but the other librarians and staff also need to learn and respect the boundaries of each role. This is a very different model from that where the Director is only an administrator.

Being Included

Some library Directors may be reluctant to be part of the campus leadership team, or there may not be a history of inviting the Director to the right "administrative table." If the Director doesn't have regular and sustained access to the people who shape policy, budget, and status on campus, then the library will likely become marginal to the real academic life of the institution. The Director must want to be included as a campus leader, and then be invited to the table. If not invited, the Director needs to subtly and persistently let the right people know that a change would be welcomed. Participating in campus leadership is basic to being a politically effective library Director. When that occurs, there are benefits to the library, but also to the campus academic agenda.

Administrator's Allegiance

For the library to be an effective part of the college or university, the library Director must be a peer and colleague of other campus administrators, especially of the Deans. Management of the library is nested in the college or university's priorities, budget, and performance. The library Director needs to be on the institution's management team at some level. How well the Director becomes a contributing member of the management team is one factor in determining the status and budget of the library. After decisions are made about institutional directions, priorities, and budgets, then library administrators need to be supportive, even when a decision conflicts with desired levels of library services.

Especially in small-staff libraries where the Director also does librarian work, the dual role of simultaneously being administrator and librarian can lead to dilemmas for the Director. For the longer-term sake of the library program, a Director/librarian needs to be allied with campus administrators. Yet, when also doing librarian work, it may be hard for other library staff to understand the Director's allegiance to the people who made decisions not supportive of the library's immediate needs (e.g., budget, staffing, or space). The Director needs to believe that being welcome at the "administrative table" is better than not being included, and continue to be strategic about improving conditions.

Campus Culture

The Director needs to intentionally learn and correctly interpret the political culture of a campus. That means understanding the recent administrative history, and the behavioral norms for administrators. Some of this is learned by watching other administrators. Other information comes from finding one or two trusted mentors who will explain things which otherwise make no sense. This is both for learning and sharing, but more importantly for understanding what is observed and what to do as a consequence.

Some insights about the campus culture come from being present at regularly scheduled meetings with an administrative group, such as the Deans. Such peer groups function as de facto clubs in an organization that probably has several de facto clubs. It is important to understand the unwritten norms and protocols of each group in order to become and remain a member in good standing. This is where the Director can become a campus insider.

Art of Compromise

The Director needs to learn how and when to compromise with other campus administrators. There are issues of money, space, and status that may be desirable for the library, but that may not be currently attainable. For the good of the institution, and for the longer-term good of the library, there are times when the Director should strategically retreat from making a request (or prolonging that request). There will be other times, or other ways, for the library to achieve what is desired, but in the near term it may be wiser to compromise and move on. Compromise is often best done in private with the Provost, saying in effect, "I don't agree, but I'll support that decision because it is best for the institution right now. In exchange, can we reopen this discussion later, or do the following when it is appropriate?"

Compromise is most easily seen in budget-making. The library budget competes with all other campus units for funds, and can be reduced by the institution's top administrators in favor of a politically higher need, or it can be increased. Departmental budgets are commonly driven by a perception shared by top administrators of the need and value that will come to the institution from that expenditure. Data is one factor, but so is the status of that unit's leader. The integrity and collegial nature of that leader are often correlated to budget decisions. For example, other administrators tire of the library Director's predictable talk about not having enough money in the library budget. Most Deans and heads of departments are likely short of money for their units. There is acquired wisdom in knowing how and when to talk about money, and when to keep quiet.

APPLICATION

Support the School

All library leaders need to be active supporters of the college or university. There are three basic ways to support the school. First, the academic library Director should attend as many campus events as possible. Like a good politician, the Director should see each campus event as an opportunity to meet new people, and greet those already known. Second, the Director needs to support the institution by being a financial contributor. One way to say "I care about this place" is to donate money. Library administrators should become annual contributors of money at a "leadership" level. Third, the Director needs to be a supporter of the school by speaking well of the school, on campus as well as off.

Initiate Meetings

A good way to build working relationships across campus is to initiate times to meet with individuals who lead departments, and with whom the Director works from time to time. Preface an invitation as something being done with other administrators. Summer is a good time for intentionally scheduling coffee or lunches with other administrators.

Meet in Office

When there is a meeting with another Dean or department head, and if the Director has a suitable office, then offer to have the meeting there. They probably don't get invited often into the library, and rarely into the Director's office. This works if the office is the equivalent size and quality of their offices. It is not as good an idea if the Director's office space is insignificant. The Director's office can be of value in making connections with other administrators.

Seek Campus Leadership Roles

It is desirable for the library Director to serve in campus leadership roles. While there is always enough to do within the library, it is good for the library's image if the Director says "yes" when asked to serve on search committees, task forces, or ongoing governance groups. On such committees the Director can help strategically position the library to play meaningful roles in various campus initiatives. It is especially important to be invited to work on institutional assessment, accreditation, and the writing of educational goals and outcomes. The Director demonstrates in such committee work that library leaders contribute more than just the predictable library perspective.

Knowing Administrative Assistants

Developing working relationships with various Administrative Assistants across campus is useful. They can either help with access to other administrators, or make it difficult. Perceptions of campus administrators are often created and shared by Administrative Assistants, and those opinions can be influential.

READING

STANDARDS AND GUIDELINES

Association of College and Research Libraries. "Standards for Libraries in Higher Education." Chicago: American Library Association, 2011. www.ala.org/acrl/standards/standardslibraries.

ADVICE AND RESEARCH

Abbott, Thomas E. "Keeping Your Library on the Right (Correct) Side of Campus Politics." In *Mistakes in Academic Library Management: Grievous Errors and How to Avoid Them,* edited by Jack E. Fritts, Jr. Lanham, MD: Scarecrow Press, 2009.

Bolman, Lee G., and Joan V. Gallos. *Reframing Academic Leadership.* San Francisco: Jossey-Bass, 2011.

Budd, John M. *The Changing Academic Library: Operations, Culture, Environments*, 2nd ed. Chicago: Association of College and Research Libraries, 2012.

Evans, G. Edward, and Patricia Layzell Ward. *Leadership Basics for Librarians and Information Professionals.* Lanham, MD: Scarecrow Press, 2007.

Heifetz, Ronald, Alexander Grashow, and Marty Linsky. *The Practice of Adaptive Leadership. Tools and Tactics for Changing Your Organization and the World.* Boston: Harvard Business Press, 2009.

Hernon, Peter, ed. *Shaping the Future. Advancing the Understanding of Leadership.* Santa Barbara, CA: Libraries Unlimited, 2010.

Hernon, Peter, Ronald R. Powell, and Arthur P. Young. "University Library Directors in the Association of Research Libraries: The Next Generation, Part One." *College & Research Libraries* 62, no. 2 (March 2001): 116–146.

Hernon, Peter, and Nancy Rossiter, eds. *Making a Difference: Leadership and Academic Libraries.* Westport, CT: Libraries Unlimited, 2007.

Library Leadership & Management Association (LLAMA). A Division of the American Library Association. www.ala.org/llama.

Mash, S. David. *Decision-Making in the Absence of Certainty. A Study in the Context of Technology and the Construction of the 21st Century Academic Library.* Chicago: American Library Association, 2011.

Rooke, David, and William R. Torbert. "Seven Transformations of Leadership." In *HBR's 10 Must Reads on Leadership.* Boston: Harvard Business Review Press, 2011.

Winston, Mark. "Leadership Research in Library and Information Science." In *Academic Library Research: Perspectives and Current Trends,* edited by Marie L. Radford, and Pamela Snelson. 189–213. Chicago: Association of College and Research Libraries, 2008.

Watkins, Michael. *The First 90 Days: Critical Success Strategies for New Leaders at All Levels.* Boston: Harvard Business Review Press, 2003.

4
Organizational Chart

The Academic Side, with Dotted Lines

ASSERTION

The academic library Director reports to an academic administrator and meets with the same group as the academic Deans.

COMMENTARY

The Academic Side

The daily work of the library staff is more connected to the academic side than to the technology, operations, or student services side of the institution. The librarians:

- are knowledgeable about the campus curriculum,
- teach information literacy,
- work with many faculty and students on research projects,
- observe how students are taught,
- serve on campus curricular and policy committees, and
- know what library resources are needed for faculty research.

Additionally, in some institutions a learning commons is part of the library, featuring tutoring, writing, math, or technology assistance. The daily work occurring in the library is part of the campus teaching, learning, and research agendas, and that is more on the academic rather than the operations side.

The Provost

The politically best situation for the academic library Director is a reporting relationship to a supervisor who can influence the budgetary and political status of the library. That is usually a leader on the academic side such as the Provost, or someone close to that level. By reporting to the Provost, the Director can talk with the Provost about the library's educational role, and what it will take financially and politically for the library to continuously reinvent its instructional strategies, resources, facilities, and services. The Director and Provost can "peer around the corner," anticipate changes, and translate that into practice.

Deans

Politically the best group for the library Director to be part of is the academic Dean's group. This is rarely a group of equals. Some academic Deans are more influential than others. Depending on the type of institution, the library Director is more or less of a peer. There is only one Director, and there are many Deans. Their responsibilities, budget, and political issues are different from those of the library Director. Nevertheless, the Director has more in common with Deans than with other administrators.

The Director needs to find good reasons to be perceived by the Deans as someone who brings useful information, observations, and insight to the group. That means talking less about predictable library-centric issues, and more about ways in which the library and its staff play roles in the teaching, learning, and research process. For example, the Director has valuable perspectives on topics such as teaching space, departmental trends in pedagogy, use of instructional technology, evaluation of teaching, changes in publishing, data collection for accreditation, user-centric web design, copyright, storage and retrieval of departmental information, data services, study abroad, and the General Education requirements. By meeting regularly with the Deans, the library director is integrated into the academic agenda, budget considerations, and campus politics. It is important that the library Director be a contributing part of the academic leadership, rather than isolated from it. The Director needs to lead a unit that is well-connected administratively to the fundamental purpose of the institution.

The Operations Side

The library is heavily dependent on the operations side of the institution, especially the departments of Facilities and Information Technology. The quality of the electronic infrastructure and the quality of the library building are foundational for the library's success. But bricks and wires shouldn't determine the library's place on the organizational chart. The question is whether the library is best situated on the academic side (curriculum, teaching, learning, research, and storing or providing access to intellectual content), or the operations side (facilities and technology). The library is dependent on the departments that manage facilities and technology, but is more closely allied with the academic agendas of teaching, learning, and research.

Dotted-Line Connections

While the best place for the library on the organizational chart is on the academic side, there are other non-academic departments to which a "dotted-line" connection is desirable for the library. On an organizational chart, solid lines connect functions and budget within the same "org." A dotted line crosses "orgs" and shows that while budgets and reporting relationships are different, nevertheless there is enough in common for individuals to have recurring meetings. Dotted-line connections can be formal or informal. Supervisors need to know that dotted-line meetings occur.

APPLICATION

Update Meeting

The best model for the reporting relationship between the academic library Director and the Provost is a recurring, biweekly, half-hour update meeting. These meetings are more about communication, leadership, and trust than they are about control. The Director should prepare a short agenda for these meetings. Some items will be FYI, and some will be for discussion. The Director needs to inform the Provost about upcoming issues so that the Provost is not surprised. The Provost should choose what other agenda items he or she wants to talk about. The Director should not bring one problem after another to the Provost, seeking guidance and help. Provosts have plenty of problems to solve. On those rare occasions when the Director must bring an issue to the Provost, it is wise to also bring one or several solutions for discussion.

In the course of the update meetings the Director will help the Provost see the full spectrum of the Director's work and the library's roles. No one else is going to do this. The Director should also be very aware of the Provost's limited time, and be sure that the meeting ends on time, regardless of when it started.

"Dotted-Line" Meetings

A recurring meeting should exist between administrators of the library and Information Technology. If they are in different orgs and report to different supervisors, then this is an example of a "dotted-line" meeting. These meetings are helpful to talk about current issues, plan for the future, and think strategically.

There are also a few library staff members who should meet regularly with their counterparts in the Information Technology group. They need to talk at the implementation level about issues, but also have detailed conversations about longer-term changes being explored. The Director should keep the Provost aware that these meetings occur.

There are leaders of other departments who should meet periodically with the library Director, or another library administrator. The Director should know people in Facilities who plan capital projects, as well as those who are responsible for custodial and maintenance issues. Often off-campus groups use the library when on campus for meetings. Catering services provide food for meetings in larger library rooms. The communications group provides access to ways of sending out information about the library, as well as doing stories on the library for campus publications. The fund-raising department can work with the Director to raise private funds.

Contribute to the Discussion

How does the library Director become valued by other administrators on the academic side? One way is for the Director to keep up with reading about trends and issues in higher education. As part of the Director's normal reading some material should be on higher education. The Director doesn't need to be authoritative on areas of specialty of other administrators, but ought to be aware of trends and issues. It is desirable to understand the context of higher education, and be able to contribute to the discussion of educational issues.

READING

STANDARDS AND GUIDELINES

Association of College and Research Libraries. "Standards for Libraries in Higher Education." Chicago: American Library Association, 2011. www.ala.org/acrl/standards/standardslibraries.

ADVICE AND RESEARCH

Alire, Camila A., and G. Edward Evans. *Academic Librarianship*. New York: Neal-Schuman Publishers, Inc., 2010.

Budd, John M. *The Changing Academic Library: Operations, Culture, Environments*, 2nd ed. Chicago: Association of College and Research Libraries, 2012.

Estabrook, Leigh S. "What Chief Academic Officers Want from Their Libraries: Findings from Interviews with Provosts and Chief Academic Officers." Chicago: Association of College and Research Libraries, 2007. www.ala.org/acrl/sites/ala.org.acrl/files/content/publications/whitepapers/Finalreport-ACRLCAOs.pdf.

Gabarro, John J., and John P. Kotter. "Managing Your Boss." In *HBR's 10 Must Reads: On Managing People*. Boston: Harvard Business Review Press, 2011.

Lambert, Leo M. "Chief Academic Officers." In *Field Guide to Academic Leadership*, edited by Robert M. Diamond, 425–435. San Francisco: Jossey-Bass, 2002.

Leaming, Deryl R. "Academic Deans." In *Field Guide to Academic Leadership*, edited by Robert M. Diamond, 437–450. San Francisco: Jossey-Bass, 2002.

Watkins, Michael. *The First 90 Days: Critical Success Strategies for New Leaders at All Levels*. Boston: Harvard Business Review Press, 2003.

5
Context

Monitoring and Interpreting Trends

ASSERTION

The academic library Director monitors the campus environment, and then interprets correctly what is seen, heard, or read in order to understand what might impact the library, and how as a consequence the library might impact the campus academic life.

COMMENTARY

Higher Education Trends

The academic library Director ought to monitor some of the literature on higher education to be aware of trends that might impact the library. This refers both to external events impacting the institution, and hence the library, but also where the library ought to play a new or expanded educational role. Is there an emerging gap between educational needs in the institution, and how the institution is staffed? If so, is the library the right unit to take on a new role? Changing student and faculty demographics, competition for students, digital teaching and learning, increasing costs of employee salaries and benefits, changes in revenue sources, changes in publishing, and trends in student majors, are examples of changes affecting higher education which may well impact a specific institution and its library. The Director not only needs to watch these changes at a national level, and local institutional level, but also talk and plan the library's response. The response may require a change within the library, or the library might strategically help to change some aspect of campus academic life.

Campus Politics

The Director needs to schedule times to get out of the office, out of the library, and into the lives of people who can become trusted sources of information about campus politics. This is harder to do in a small-staff library where the Director is a librarian and administrator. The goal is information beyond what is learned in structured meetings. E-mails won't replace the need to personally know people who have reliable inside information, and who will talk about incidents, emerging perceptions, and coming issues. Learning how to interpret campus politics requires a wise confidant, the willingness to learn from errors in judgment, and plenty of time to build trust with insiders. Like a historian, the Director needs to understand the perspectives of various contacts, and the sources of their information. Context matters, and there are often several layers to adequately understand a situation. In the meantime, watch, ask, listen, think, and stay humble.

The Neighborhood

The library exists in the context of the campus, but also within the neighborhood where the institution is located. How does that neighborhood affect the library? There might be an institutional effort to welcome neighbors onto campus, and hence access to the library might be part of that. If so, then there are procedural implications, such as access to the campus's hardwired and wireless network. Or, campus policy might restrict access to buildings to those with a campus identification card, in which case admittance to the library might be through a staffed entrance or via a security card system. The campus position about non-students is usually a high-level policy decision. The Director and library staff need to figure out procedurally how to implement such.

APPLICATION
Daily Walks

The academic library Director ought to walk through the library several times each day, with his or her "antenna" tuned to a wide variety of images in order to understand what external factors impact the library. For example:

- Which students are using what parts of the library and during what time of day?
- Are there non-students in the library, and if so, who are they and why are they there?
- Is there graffiti, and if so, what does that mean?
- Are spaces used in ways that support the academic image of the library?
- Are there signs taped to walls as if the library was a public billboard?

There are countless details to notice and then evaluate in order to decide if they mean anything about campus attitudes or issues which might affect the library.

Ethnographic Research

There are ways to use social science techniques to understand who uses what parts of the library, what services, at what time of what days, and what this could mean for changes in the library. There is also research on how students use or don't use specific libraries, resources, and librarians. Some of that could be replicated locally, to understand gaps between what the library offers and what faculty and students actually use. To understand local practice, there might be faculty interested in involving a class in collecting and analyzing data, from fields as different as marketing, interior design, architecture, anthropology, sociology, and statistics. Library student workers could walk around the library and document usage. While trying to understand student patterns of library use is labor intensive, nevertheless, scaling a project to what can realistically be done might be useful. Such ethnographic research can provide the underpinning for decisions, such as the library's hours of operation, rearrangement of space, or a renewed emphasis on some aspect of information literacy.

Curricular Committees

A library Director needs a staff member on undergraduate and graduate curricular and policy committees. That is one way to learn about the evolving direction of the curriculum (e.g., new courses, programs, certificates, and degrees), and any other changes in policy or procedures that will impact the library. Such committees also conduct program reviews of departments. That is a very good time to assess the alignment of the library with a specific department or program.

Institutional Data

A college or university has an office responsible for institutional data. This is the source of reports on demographic trends, enrollment, surveys, and a wide variety of other topics. The library Director needs the same level of access to this data as academic Deans in order to understand trends that impact the library, such as number of students in each major or degree program, number of transfer students, or class size. There is usually a wealth of data about an institution's current students, including results from assessments such as the National Survey of Student Engagement (NSSE), the Community College Survey of Student Engagement (CCSSE), the Faculty Survey of Student Engagement (FSSE), and the Collegiate Learning Assessment (CLA).

Higher Education Reading

As part of a library administrator's daily reading, it is good to include the *Chronicle of Higher Education*, EDUCAUSE, CLIR publications, and any other journals, blogs, or RSS feeds which report on news and trends of interest to a campus. Additionally, it is wise for the library to develop a book collection on higher education history and policy, focused particularly on similar schools. When one of these books enters the library collection, it should be routed to the Director for a quick look. The Director may be able to play a useful role for Deans and other administrators by commenting on a new higher education book and even supplying a copy.

READING

STANDARDS AND GUIDELINES

Association of College and Research Libraries. "Standards for Libraries in Higher Education." Chicago: American Library Association, 2011. www.ala.org/acrl/standards/standardslibraries.

ADVICE AND RESEARCH

ACRL Research Planning and Review Committee. "2012 Top Ten Trends in Academic Libraries: A Review of the Current Literature." *College & Research Libraries News* 73 no. 6, (June 2012): 311–320. http://crln.acrl.org/content/73/6/311.full.pdf+html.

ACRL Research Planning and Review Committee. "Environmental Scan 2013." Chicago: Association of College and Research Libraries, 2013. www.ala.org/acrl/sites/ala.org.acrl/files/content/publications/whitepapers/EnvironmentalScan13.pdf.

Alire, Camila A., and G. Edward Evans. *Academic Librarianship*. New York: Neal-Schuman Publishers, Inc., 2010.

AnthroLib. River Campus Libraries | University of Rochester. https://urresearch.rochester.edu/viewInstitutionalCollection.action?collectionId=217.

Budd, John M. *The Changing Academic Library: Operations, Culture, Environments*, 2nd ed. Chicago: Association of College and Research Libraries, 2012.

Chronicle of Higher Education. http://chronicle.com.

Council on Library and Information Resources. www.clir.org.

Educause. www.educause.edu.

Foster, Nancy Fried, and Susan Gibbons, eds. *Studying Students: The Undergraduate Research Project at the University of Rochester*. Chicago: Association of College and Research Libraries, 2007.

Maloney, Krisellen, Kristin Antelman, Kenning Arlitsch, and John Butler. "Future Leaders' Views on Organizational Culture." *College & Research Libraries* 71, no. 4 (July 2010): 322–347.

"Participatory Design in Academic Libraries: Methods, Findings, and Implementations." Washington, DC: Council on Library and Information Resources, 2012.

Staley, David, and Kara Malenfant. Futures Thinking for Academic Librarians: Higher Education in 2025. Chicago: Association of College and Research Libraries, 2010. www.ala.org/acrl/sites/ala.org.acrl/files/content/issues/value/futures2025.pdf.

Wood, Elizabeth J., Rush Miller, and Amy Knapp. *Beyond Survival: Managing Academic Libraries in Transition*. Westport, CT: Libraries Unlimited, 2007.

6

Academic Ceiling

Dependencies and Levels of Quality

ASSERTION

The academic library Director understands that the quality of the library is heavily determined by the institution's "academic ceiling," the level at which institutional leaders set budgets and expectations, including for those units upon which the library is dependent.

COMMENTARY

Academic Ceiling

Academic library administrators and staff need to decide the content and services that the library can realistically provide, and at what level. What library services and content do faculty, students, and campus administrators really want? Is that the same list as what librarians want to provide? How close can the library come to providing all of these, and at what level of quality?

A basic step in answering those questions is determining the level of the "academic ceiling" in the college or university. The "academic ceiling" is a level of quality determined by the intersection of the institutional budget and the aspirations of each unit, from academics and athletics to facilities and student activities. The institutional budget is driven by judgments made by top administrators about the priority of competing needs and wants. Determining the academic ceiling level begins with mission and goal statements, a strategic plan, and includes judgments from the governing board, faculty, and students.

The library's ability to provide content and services is capped by the level of its own budget, as well as the budgets of departments upon which the library is dependent. As examples of dependencies, the quality of the campus network, wiring, and computing equipment within the library is important, but those are normally the business of the institution's Information Technology and Facilities departments. Their budgets and priorities will determine the level of wired and wireless access in the library. Or, the library may need capital improvements, but such remodeling projects are approved, funded, and managed by departments other than the library. The ceiling on the level at which the library operates is determined by multiple factors, many outside the control of the library Director.

The "academic ceiling" is an evolving consensus among top administrators about the inter-connectedness of all the factors that define the institution, and their priority. The quality of the library is one of many factors. It is not an independent variable. It is, however, often a proxy indicator of the academic quality of the college or university.

Dependencies upon Other Departments

The library is not an independent department within the college or university, and the Director does not have control over all the factors that contribute to the success of the library. Rather, the library is dependent on some other departments, which are usually in different budget and reporting lines.

The library is usually dependent on the Facilities department for the:

- current condition of the library (maintenance),
- routine custodial and cleaning services, and
- capital expenditures to remodel space and upgrade systems such as electrical and HVAC.

The library is usually dependent on Information Technology for the:

- development and maintenance of the network, both throughout the campus and within the library,
- computers,
- enterprise software,
- networked print, copy, scan services, and
- policy decisions about access to the campus network.

Consequently, the relationship between the library Director and the leaders of these other departments is important to the success of the library. Such departments either have the ability to make basic parts of the library quite good, or keep them from meeting expectations, either by choice ("Not my problem") or because of a lack of financial resources ("Get in line. It's a long one").

Calibrating Quality

If expectations from campus administrators and library-using faculty are about the same as the library staff can deliver, then there is approximate agreement on those services and at what level. However, if expectations for library services from library-using departments are higher than the library can realistically deliver, then the level of the "academic ceiling" has been defined for that department. It is the Director's job to continuously understand the gap between the academic ceiling and expectations of academic departments. The quality of library services is calibrated department by department, and needs to be reviewed annually. Where there is a gap, then the Director needs to determine what can be done without becoming a tiresome critic of the institution's budget.

Campus Contracts and Departments

It is politically advantageous to use existing campus contracts and departments to supply equipment and services to the library. It is not wise to replicate campus-wide services by having someone in the library do a task which is already offered by a campus contract or department. As examples, the library need not purchase items (e.g., computers, enterprise software, and office supplies) or provide services (e.g., printing and copying, cleaning, and server space) on its own, even if it appears that it will save money or improve services. Ideally, library staff time should be spent on tasks which are not otherwise offered by a campus contract or department.

It is not worth the chance of being thought less of by other campus administrators because the library has gone outside of existing campus contracts or departments. The political price will be higher than one might anticipate. Other administrators may not forget that the library worked around existing arrangements, and in that instance wasn't on the campus team. It is better to be perceived as being on the team rather than as independent and isolated.

APPLICATION

Response to Academic Ceiling

If the institutional "academic ceiling" is below the level of library content and services desired by library administrators and librarians, and if that is not satisfactory, then there are several courses of action. One is to reallocate parts of the library budget to expenditures of higher political value. That means being clear with some faculty about what is being reallocated and why. Working within the faculty governance structure may be helpful. The academic library Director may also work with various campus departmental leaders to improve services to the library. That includes supporting budget improvements for other departments whose performance directly impacts the library, such as Information Technology and Facilities.

Computers

The quality of the computers in a library matters to the staff, and to the students who aren't using their own laptops or tablets. Library staff time should not duplicate what the Information Technology department does campus-wide for computers, namely:

- define the computer replacement cycle,
- define the specifications,
- purchase,
- install,
- maintain, and
- dispose.

For specialized computing devices beyond what is provided centrally, library staff should evaluate, purchase, and maintain such equipment. If centralized technology services aren't adequate for the library, then the Director needs to try various approaches before doing those tasks in-house.

Copy, Print, and Scan Services

The best level of service for machines that copy, print, and scan is usually obtained by letting the campus department in charge of such machines also be in charge of those in the library. This should be part of the institutional fleet contract. There is no compelling reason why library staff should lease, maintain, and pay for these machines, outside of the campus contract.

Card Services

Students sometimes need to make payments in the library (e.g., fees, fines, copying, or purchasing items). It is best to let the department on campus that manages student payments also manage library payments, and use a card system rather than accepting cash from students. It is highly desirable that library staff cease taking cash for such things as copying, printing, and paying fines. Maintaining cash registers requires staff time, and leaves room for error or theft. It is best to use existing services, especially if students are used to paying for goods and services through a campus card.

Working with Departments and Groups

The library can provide small-scale services to various campus departments and groups, most of which are short-term. For example, the library may have large rooms for end-of-term group tutoring with a specific department or with athletic teams. The Admissions department may want to bring prospective students and their parents into the library as part of the recruitment process. The student government leaders may have ideas for library space (e.g., providing newspaper racks and giving away copies of national newspapers). Residential student staff may have book study groups and need quantities of books organized, checked out, and kept during vacations. An Art department may need space for an end-of-term show. Many classes need space for poster sessions. Without giving library space away long-term, there are short-term ways to connect with departments and groups, which not only help the department but also make the library valuable from their perspectives.

READING

STANDARDS AND GUIDELINES

Association of College and Research Libraries. "Standards for Libraries in Higher Education." Chicago: American Library Association, 2011. www.ala.org/acrl/standards/standardslibraries.

ADVICE AND RESEARCH

Bunnell, David P. "Collaboration in Small and Medium-Sized Academic Libraries." In *Defining Relevancy: Managing the New Academic Library,* edited by Janet McNeil Hurlbert. Westport, CT: Libraries Unlimited, 2008.

7
Faculty

Gatekeepers of Library Usage

ASSERTION

The academic library Director reinforces with all library staff that faculty members have considerable influence with students and campus administrators in determining the use and status of the library.

COMMENTARY

Faculty As Gatekeepers

Faculty are gatekeepers for student use of the library. If specific uses of the library space, resources, and staff are written into a course syllabus and the course management software, then students will become increasingly adept at finding and using the kind of information that has been vetted and is available in and through the library. Conversely, student use of the library will be minimal if an instructor is silent or passive about using the library.

Positive Experiences

Faculty will be supportive of the library when they see examples of how those who work in the library, what is in the building, the library technology, and what is available through the website, are part of the learning or research of their students. Faculty will also be library supporters when some aspect of the library is part of their own research and publication. Faculty who use the library for their own work may well be more likely to encourage students to also use the library databases and licensed journals.

How faculty are treated by library staff, what they observe in the library, and their satisfaction with access to library content and space, all have consequences for shaping a positive or negative image of the library. Many instructors will go out of their way to plan assignments with the help of a trusted librarian. They will also pass along compliments about the importance of the library (and certain librarians) in the learning of their students, all of which reflect well on the whole library team. Conversely, poor experiences are remembered, form negative impressions, and become reasons not to include a library component in a class. The academic library Director needs to shape a library culture in which everyone understands that student use of the library is correlated to faculty satisfaction with library experiences. That has implications for the political status of the library.

Librarians As Communicators

Effective communication to faculty about library business should be done by librarians, and rarely by a library administrator. If the librarians are organized in a liaison librarian model, in which each librarian has responsibility for certain content areas, then that librarian needs to build and sustain working relationships with faculty in those academic departments. It is these librarians who will be listened to by "their" faculty when there is something necessary to communicate. The degree to which a librarian is known, valued, and trusted by faculty in an academic department is the degree to which that librarian can effectively communicate a library message, either formally or through informal influence.

Effective written communication from a librarian to faculty uses shared norms about how faculty in a particular discipline tend to write and understand those words. It begins with e-mails which are infrequent, precise, and short. It uses words and terms commonly accepted in that department. It is good for library administrators and librarians to talk about how best to communicate what kind of content and with what faculty. Norms for writing might well be summarized in an in-house style guide.

New Faculty

New faculty will bring previous library experiences ranging from superb to indifferent, so it is wise for librarians to take the initiative, meet new faculty, and create a positive initial impression. It is also desirable for all librarians to use the same structured process in introducing new faculty to library services and content, and how best to work with the librarian. The role of a library administrator is to set the expectation that introductory occasions need to occur between librarians and new faculty.

Part-Time Faculty

The same library orientation given to new faculty should also be offered to part-time faculty. There are often quite a few instructors in this category, and while the investment of librarian time may seem considerable, it is nevertheless worthwhile. Part-time faculty give assignments which may impact the library. Some of those assignments could be more successful with prior collaboration between faculty and a librarian. Offering librarian support to part-time instructors can help with a course, but can also have a longer-term impact if and when they become full-time faculty.

APPLICATION

Faculty Support of Library

Within a department there are often expectations which affect library usage. Faculty add value to their courses when there is a departmental consensus written in syllabi that:

- Students are expected to read considerably for the course (and what they are expected to read is defined in a syllabus), and that the material is available through the library.
- Librarian instruction (in-person or web-based) in some aspect of information literacy is part of the class.
- Students are expected to meet with librarians and talk about research projects.
- Students are expected to use library spaces such as a writing center, a learning commons, or a technology studio to make products of their learning.

The library experience can add value to a student's education. That is more likely to occur if faculty write expectations and learning outcomes for using the library into the class syllabus and not just leave it to the student's initiative.

New Faculty Orientation

There are several ways a librarian can welcome new faculty before the Autumn term begins. When a faculty member is hired, the librarian for that discipline should send an introductory e-mail. When that person moves into an office, that librarian should go there and make an introduction. If new faculty participate in an orientation to the institution, then it is helpful for the librarians to be on that orientation schedule. The purpose should be simple: introduce librarians and their subject areas, talk about librarian contributions to student learning, hand out something which has names and contact information, and mention follow-up visits. Subsequently, a librarian should schedule time with the new faculty member in the librarian's office to go over a checklist of what the faculty member should know about using this library and to place words in a syllabus about integrating the use of the library into their courses. Additionally, this is the time to talk about the new faculty member's research interests. Some libraries provide lunch for this orientation between new faculty and librarians. The academic library administrator's role is to see that multiple events are organized so that initial contacts are actually made between librarians and new faculty. The same holds true for faculty who are new during terms other than Autumn.

Checklists

It is helpful for librarians to offer faculty a checklist of options for ways in which the librarian can co-teach parts of a course. For example, one choice might be embedding the librarian in the course management software so that students have virtual access to an additional teacher. Or, the librarian could teach part of a session to the whole class, or to multiple small groups, in the library or the classroom. Additionally, students could view short web-based tutorials or webinars, chosen from a menu, to prepare them for a research project. The instructor should choose such options from a checklist, and customize the use of the librarian's time, knowledge, and access to resources.

READING

ADVICE AND RESEARCH

Alire, Camila A., and G. Edward Evans. *Academic Librarianship.* New York: Neal-Schuman Publishers, Inc., 2010.

Arendt, Julie, and Megan Lotts. "What Liaisons Say about Themselves and What Faculty Say about Their Liaisons, a U.S. Survey." *portal: Libraries and the Academy* 12, no. 2 (April 2012), 155–177.

Arum, Richard, and Josipa Roksa. *Academically Adrift: Limited Learning on College Campuses*. Chicago: University of Chicago Press, 2011.

"Frontline Advocacy for Academic Libraries." Chicago: American Library Association. www.ala.org/advocacy/advleg/advocacyuniversity/frontline_advocacy/frontline_academic.

McAdoo, Monty L. *Building Bridges: Connecting Faculty, Students, and the College Library*. Chicago: American Library Association, 2010.

Nicol, Erica Carlson, and Mark O'English. "Rising Tides: Faculty Expectations of Library Websites." *portal: Libraries and the Academy* 12, no. 4 (October 2012), 371–386.

Schonfeld, Roger C., and Ross Housewright. "Ithaka S+R Faculty Survey 2009: Key Strategic Insights for Libraries, Publishers, and Societies," 2009. www.sr.ithaka.org/research-publications/faculty-survey-2009.

8
Unexpected Events

Planning for Safety and Security

ASSERTION

The academic library Director is accountable to the institution's top leadership for the preparedness and response of library staff to all incidents affecting the safety and security of the library staff, patrons, building, and collections.

COMMENTARY

Staff and Patron Safety

The academic library Director's daily reality of worrying about safety never goes away, regardless of the library's location or student demographics. The campus police department is charged with preparing for employee and patron safety. The Director should meet annually with someone from the campus police and review planning for safety and security, and then do what is advised. Take seriously the preparation of the library staff for any issue which could jeopardize the safety of staff and patrons. Make sure that the staff (including student workers) are trained on how to deal with a difficult or dangerous patron, and how to respond when the police take over the campus or the library building.

Weather-Related Issues

Staff and patron safety also includes the reaction to weather-related closures, and building system failures. When the electricity goes off, a storm hits, or an earthquake occurs, then all staff need to know how to help patrons exit the building or where in the building to gather. All should know who makes a decision to evacuate and close the building. It is especially important to be clear about responsibility in the evening, on weekends, and during vacation periods. Prepare for realistic contingencies, write down those steps, print and distribute them, and make sure that all library staff know what is expected of them in emergencies.

Contents within Building

There are two safety and security issues related to contents within the building; namely, theft and damage to the building and its contents from fire or water.

- Theft

If you suspect theft of materials, then you need to work with the campus police. Do not try to investigate on your own.

- Damage

A plan for responding to water or fire damage needs to be reviewed annually. That means a clear understanding with someone in the Facilities department about what to do, who makes that decision, and who pays for it. The Director needs to understand how the sprinkler system in the library works, whether it is wet or dry, and the basis on which someone can attest that the system still works properly. Figure out whom to call if there is water damage, and keep that information up-to-date.

Who Is in Charge?

The Director needs to clearly designate who is in charge when the Director is not in the building. There must always be one employee clearly in charge of the building, and who has been trained on what to do in case of safety or security issues. Be reluctant to leave the library open with only undergraduate student workers as staff, but, if that occurs, make clear plans for an emergency response by campus police.

APPLICATION

Campus Police

It is smart for various library staff to know the campus police, and be known by them. The academic library Director and other library administrators need to know the key people within the campus police department. The people who staff the library, especially the circulation desk, need to know individual officers. Those who work at night and on weekends especially need to know the officers. The campus police need to feel welcome to walk through the library, and chat with the staff.

Emergency Closures

When there is an emergency that closes the library, then all staff need the same information so there is clarity about closure and reopening:

- Identify who makes the decision to close (or close early).
- Set guidelines for when a decision on closure is made (especially for weekends).
- Determine how a decision to close (or a decision to open after being closed) is communicated to staff.
- Have written language about the impact on salaries or annual leave of weather-related reasons for not being at work.

Security Cameras

The library Director and the head of the campus security department need to decide on the wisdom of placing security cameras in the library and their location. Generally, the library should have security cameras at the entrances and in strategic places on each floor. The images from these cameras should be available at the desktop computers of several key staff, as well as in the campus security office. The purpose of security cameras is the safety of patrons and staff. The placement of cameras needs to be for safety, and hence minimize their intrusion upon patron privacy.

Access to Library

There are two issues regarding safety and security when considering access to the library building. One is a perception of safety for students. Some academic libraries are open to the public, but others staff the entrance so that only those with campus identification can enter the building. The other issue is access at night and on weekends. Some buildings have doors which open with a campus identification card, and hence students can gain access after regular staff have gone home. During these late-night hours the library can be staffed at a minimal level, but should not be unstaffed. While some small libraries use only student workers in the evenings, that is a decision the Director should make in consultation with the campus police and Provost. Keeping the library open and staffing it only with student workers is a decision usually driven by salary cost. However, if a serious incident occurred and only student workers were on site, then that could be an especially regrettable decision.

Collection Preservation

The Director needs to work with someone from Facilities on issues relating to preservation of the collections, such as the temperature and humidity in the building, and the need for special environments for fragile formats. Some of this is for everyday long-term preservation, but it also includes awareness of what to do if the sprinkler system is activated. Think through daily operations as well as contingencies with someone from Facilities, and write this down. The same conversation should occur with someone from Information Technology about the library's electronic infrastructure. Make sure everyone is clear about what is backed up, and how. Make sure that the right people from the library and the Information Technology department understand how to keep digital material safe and backed up, and what to do in an emergency.

READING

STANDARDS AND GUIDELINES

Association of College and Research Libraries. "Standards for Libraries in Higher Education." Chicago: American Library Association, 2011. www.ala.org/acrl/standards/standardslibraries.

ADVICE AND RESEARCH

Alire, Camila A., and G. Edward Evans. *Academic Librarianship*. New York: Neal-Schuman Publishers, 2010.

Alire, Camila, ed. *Library Disaster Planning and Recovery Handbook*. New York: Neal-Schuman, 2000.

"Disaster Response: A Selected Annotated Bibliography. ALA Fact Sheet 10." Chicago: American Library Association, 2006. www.ala.org/Template .cfm?Section=libraryfactsheet&Template=/ContentManagement/ ContentDisplay.cfm&ContentID=25420.

Thomas, Marcia. *Emergency Response Planning in College Libraries.* CLIP Note #40. Chicago: Association of College and Research Libraries, 2009.

Kahn, Miriam B. *Disaster Response and Planning for Libraries,* 3rd ed. Chicago: American Library Association, 2012.

Kahn, Miriam. *The Library Security and Safety Guide to Prevention, Planning, and Response.* Chicago: American Library Association, 2008.

LLAMA BES Safety & Security of Library Buildings Committee. "Library Security Guidelines Document." Chicago: American Library Association, 2010. www.ala .org/llama/sites/ala.org.llama/files/content/publications/LibrarySecurity Guide.pdf.

Wilkinson, Frances C., Linda K. Lewis, and Nancy K. Dennis. *Comprehensive Guide to Emergency and Disaster Preparedness and Recovery.* Chicago: American Library Association, 2009.

PART II
Managing and Leading Staff

Part II consists of topics on managing and leading the library staff. This is the hard part of being an academic library administrator. Staff members come and go, attitudes and morale change, events from personal lives affect job performance, technology changes job duties, and expectations from campus administrators can create staffing dilemmas. The pieces of this puzzle are always moving. However, for those times when the right people are in place and doing their work effectively, then managing and leading staff are very gratifying parts of an administrator's job.

9
Beginning

Starting a New Position

ASSERTION

An academic library administrator begins a new position in ways that have important implications for the rest of the tenure.

COMMENTARY

Inherited Context

When beginning an administrative position, it is essential to understand the context that a predecessor or predecessors left, and hence the images people carry over and now put on the new person, the library, and the work they expect. Rarely does anyone start a new position with a clean page or screen. Images and expectations have already been created. Each staff member was hired by another administrator. Everyone has a story about why things are the way they are.

It is wise for a new academic library administrator to spend the first few months from the perspective of a historian in order to understand what and who has been inherited. Listen, question ("What do I need to know?"), and correlate these responses, but don't offer judgments back to the people willing to tell their stories. You are likely viewed and heard differently among the employees, depending on what individuals think you can and will do to their work conditions.

At some point, as a new administrator, you will have learned enough, and should cease being a historian. Keep in mind advice like: "Be a historian. Quit being a historian," and know when too many stories from the past continue to define the present. You need to say to yourself: "Enough. I get it. I don't need to hear more of these stories." Understand how the past created the present, but do not let the past define the next steps. Only after understanding the impact of previous people and their actions on the library's present will you have a chance to shape new realities and images for a new tenure.

Success

It is in the self-interest of a lot of people that a new administrator is successful, and that is why it matters how one starts. It cost the institution some money, time, and emotional energy to search for and hire this person. Various faculty, staff, and administrators spent their time evaluating applications, interviewing, and making a decision. The school may even have paid moving expenses. Time, money, and reputations are intertwined in this hiring. No one wants to be wrong and have to re-do the search in a few years. It will also cost people their time and emotional energy to bring a new person into their work lives. Consequently, the library staff, the library-using faculty, the Deans, the heads of various departments, the Provost, and even the President all want the new administrator to succeed, and to succeed sooner rather than later. It is in the self-interest of many people that a new administrator learns how things are done, builds good relationships, does well, and stays awhile.

Meet People

The two top priorities for any new library administrator in the first academic year are to meet and get to know as many as possible of the:

- library staff; and
- faculty, staff, and administrators.

While an administrator needs to quickly learn the details of the job, it is foundational to learn the personal stories and work strengths of the people around him or her. Even in a large university it is important to meet and know something about all the people who work in the library. Meeting and getting to know the people one works with is the foundation for any administrator's subsequent success.

In addition to knowing library staff, the academic library Director needs to know as many people in other campus departments as possible. The Director has to take the initiative to do that, especially in the first few months. If the Director doesn't get outside of the library and meet other campus administrators, staff, and some faculty in their offices, then the Director will pay the ongoing price of being less-than-visible. Make connections, and be seen as the leader of the library.

Overview of Procedures

Library administrators at any level are fortunate if the institution provides formal workshops on how to do certain tasks. For example, it is in everyone's self-interest if an administrator understands the process for making and spending the budget, and using the financial software. In some places an individual doesn't receive access to the financial software until completing a workshop. An orientation to procedures used by Human Resources or the Facilities department is equally useful. New administrators will figure these things out on their own, and over time, but it is so much smarter if the institution provides a formal overview early in an administrator's tenure.

Symbolic Transfer

Success in managing a library staff begins with establishing a working relationship with each employee. What that means depends on the size of the staff. With a large staff it may only mean an initial introduction, and the Director's effort to remember a name and say "hello" when walking around. With a smaller staff the Director can indeed be introduced to each employee. While a formal introduction to all employees takes a fair amount of time, it is nevertheless worthwhile. It makes a strong symbolic statement that work relationships are foundational to a well-managed library, and that a transfer has occurred from one administrator to another.

Pacing

The Director may have a lot of "first impressions," and may want to get started right away on making some changes. However, many things take more time to change than is apparent. Some changes may require getting on the list of tasks to be done by a particular department, such as Information Technology, Facilities, or Human Resources. Others require understanding the story behind why things are as they are and the implications of making any change. Change may also require understanding the inherited governance process, and first either clarifying or changing how decisions will be made. In short, before attempting any changes, it is smart to first understand:

- the process used by campus departments to determine what work to do next,
- the history of what you observe, and
- the library's inherited decision-making process.

Additionally, any initial sense of pacing what needs to be done is related to a longer-term need for clarity about mission, goals, and a plan to achieve them. First impressions need to be tempered by clarity about mission, goals, and a strategic plan.

APPLICATION

Wince List

The "wince list" is the academic library Director's private list of negative first impressions. It is smart to keep a list, and take some time to understand the history of what caused the wince, and the process for making a change. There are likely more items on the list than there is time, money, or political capital to deal with, at least initially. Nevertheless, if all those initial puzzling spaces, objects, procedures, attitudes, and people are noted on a private list, then over time many of them will likely be changed. If they are initially not put on a wince list, then some will become familiar, overlooked, and never dealt with.

Administrator Mentor

A successful library Director takes the initiative in order to build as many working relationships across campus as possible in the first year. Indeed, it is very desirable if the institution has a formal way of helping the Director make those connections. For example, a new Director may be assigned a mentor who is an administrator in another part of the institution. Hopefully there are scheduled times with the leaders of other campus departments. A good campus mentor introduces the Director around to others, including informally.

Three-Person Introduction

One effective way for the Director to make a good first impression is to be introduced personally to each employee. In a smaller library this can occur with short individual meetings, and in a larger library it might occur in departmental meetings of several people. If the previous Director is available, then that person could host the introduction of the new Director to employees.

One effective technique is a three-person introductory meeting. The employee prepares a one-page template about him or herself. The outgoing Director uses this to lead a three-way introductory conversation with the incoming Director and the new employee. This is a symbolic transfer, but it also gives the new Director a brief overview of each employee (e.g., current work tasks, history in the library, and any appropriate personal background).

Student Employee Introductions

It is highly desirable that the new Director is introduced to each student employee, so that subsequently they can at least say "hello." It may not be customary for student workers to meet the Director, and may evoke comments about "having to go to the principal's office." The results are usually surprisingly worth everyone's time. Being acquainted with the student workers is very good for the Director personally. It is about the only way the Director will know any students. It is also good for the Director's image among the student workers and their friends. Symbolically, being introduced to student workers indicates that in a well-managed workplace, the Director knows everyone, including the student employees. Each student employee should fill out a one-page template ahead of time, which is then used in a conversation about where he or she is from, academic majors, aspirations after graduation, and anything else that seems appropriate.

Director's Office

A new Director needs to establish an identity distinct from the previous Director, and one way to do that which doesn't need permission or advice from anyone is to change the look of the office. Leftover hints of a predecessor should not linger because the unchanged interior reminds staff of who used to work there. Usually someone in Facilities will assist in changing the variables of:

- color (paint the walls),
- position (rearrange the desk and chairs),
- furniture (obtain a different desk, chairs, table, area rug, or shelving),
- light (add or remove lamps),
- plants (add or remove large plants),
- technology (add a flat screen to the wall, or multiple screens on your desk, or remove all the screens from your desk), and
- art (hang art on the walls).

READING

STANDARDS AND GUIDELINES

Association of College and Research Libraries. "Standards for Libraries in Higher Education." Chicago: American Library Association, 2011. www.ala.org/acrl/standards/standardslibraries.

ADVICE AND RESEARCH

Watkins, Michael. *The First 90 Days: Critical Success Strategies for New Leaders at All Levels*. Boston: Harvard Business Review Press, 2003.

10
The Job

Nature of Administrative Work

ASSERTION

An academic library administrator is both a leader and a manager, and this dual role must be understood in the same way by the administrator, the supervisor, and the library staff.

COMMENTARY

Leader and Manager

Being an effective academic library administrator begins with being both a leader and a manager. In a manager's role the administrator cares about influencing the conditions under which other staff can do their work well. The manager asks: "Is the library or department correctly staffed, is the budget being spent on the right things, are the work procedures clear, are the staff trained, and is the work done at the right level of quality?" In a leadership role the administrator is more attuned to what tasks should be done, and by whom, and especially in an environment where the college, university, and library all deal with ongoing change. A leader wonders: "Why is this task being done at all, is the right person doing the work, and should something else be done instead?" A leader thinks about how the library fits into the institution's educational role, and hence what should be done in the library to fulfill that role. An academic library administrator plays the dual role of being both a manager and leader.

Director's Supervisor

The academic library Director reports to the Provost, is accountable to the Provost, and hence must pay attention to what the Provost thinks the library needs to do (and with what resources). The library Director and all who work in the library need to understand that the definition of the library, and what that means in terms of each person's role, may well change as a function of priorities from the supervisor. The Director may bring certain expectations, and the staff may have contract language, job descriptions, or aspirations. However, the Director has a supervisor, and that person likely has certain expectations. For example, the expectations from the Provost to the Director might be:

Resolve specific issues: "There are these identified issues, and I hired you to resolve them."

Continue on the current direction: "The library is fine as it is. Manage the daily operation with the resources you have. I did not hire you to make big changes."

Be a change agent: "We're spending a lot of money on the library and the data shows that we're not getting much use out of our annual investment. Figure out why the libraries at comparable schools are more effective than our library. Help us understand where academic libraries are headed in upcoming years. Let's build a plan to make our library exemplary. I hired you to be a change agent."

The Director and the staff need to understand that they are not autonomous, but that the library is nested within the institution's budget, buildings, labor agreements, electronic infrastructure, status relative to comparable schools, and overall self-image. A number of factors and people have influence over the library. The Director and the staff are not making strategic decisions independently.

Director's Accountability

The Provost may not intervene in the management of the library, but the Provost does hold the Director accountable for everything related to the operation of the library, such as:

- the budget,
- personnel,
- policy and procedures,
- intellectual content,
- information literacy,
- the building,
- the website,
- planning for emergencies, and
- the library systems software.

In some areas the Director is an advocate for the library, sharing responsibility with another department, such as Facilities, Human Resources, or Information Technology. In other areas the Director and staff have primary responsibility. The Director is the "quality control" person, always asking, observing, and evaluating all aspects of library operation, knowing that accountability eventually falls to him or her.

Variables of Size and Research Emphasis

The enrollment of the institution, and the emphasis on research and publication, drive the size of the library staff and their job duties. Those two variables in turn determine the Director's role. The National Center for Educational Statistics reported that in 2012 there were 3,793 academic libraries. Of those, 1,388 were in institutions with less than 1,000 FTE enrollment. In a high percentage of these libraries the total size of the staff was small enough so that the Director worked as both a librarian and as the administrator of the library. Additionally, 1,507 libraries were in institutions that granted the Associate degree. Community colleges and many smaller colleges have a dominant emphasis on teaching rather than faculty research and publication.

The two factors of enrollment size and research emphasis usually drive how academic libraries are organized, budgeted for, and managed. In libraries with small staffs, the Director has the dual role of administrator and librarian, and hence will likely teach, do collection management, or reference. There is limited time for meetings within and outside the library. The administrator/librarian has fewer opportunities for political influence among other campus administrators. Managing and evaluating the several other library staff require skills and wisdom of a different nature than from those who administer large staffs. The focus of the administrator/librarian and others on the staff is predominantly working directly with students and faculty. The nature of the Director's work is the Director's decision, and needs to be determined by the value of doing a certain amount of librarian work judged against other administrative tasks that the Director must also do.

Other Library Administrators

Depending on the size and organization of the library, there are others with administrative responsibilities for daily operations. The Director needs to delegate some tasks and responsibilities to other library administrators, but then stay aware of how things are going in those delegated areas. The Director is still accountable for tasks delegated or shared. The Director's job includes recurring update meetings with other administrators and managers, so that there are no surprises about anything occurring in the library. The Director cannot let a situation develop where some staff try to manipulate and use middle management, and in the process work against the library goals, specific projects, daily procedures, or some individuals. Other administrators help make policy and procedures, but equally important, shape opinions among staff and carry out agreed-upon policy and procedures. These administrative positions are also where future directors are mentored and prepared for leadership roles.

Collaboration and Accountability

The librarians and staff have defined ways for collaborating with administrators on many decisions. Nevertheless, the Director is accountable for decisions (however made) affecting all aspects of the library's operation. There may be a history and culture of collaboration, but the Provost will look at results more than process. When something goes wrong, the Director is accountable to the Provost and will need to provide answers to "What happened?" and "Why did you allow certain decisions that created this situation?" It is not a sufficient answer for the Director to say "The librarians voted the wrong way, over my better judgment," or to blame a decision made by a predecessor or another department. Collaborative decision-making may be an institutional and library staff norm, but in the view of a results-oriented Provost the Director is ultimately accountable for everything relating to the operation of the library.

Directors "Need to Know"

If the Director is accountable for what occurs in the library, then the Director needs to be clear with all library staff and administrators that potentially everything related to the operation of the library can become the Director's business. Hence, staff need to know what information must be shared with the Director and when. From the beginning of a Director's tenure, staff with responsibilities for budget, personnel, and policy need to tell the Director everything they know that the Director must know. It is not acceptable if the Director is surprised by something from the past, or something occurring in the present, simply because no one spoke up. The Director always needs to be aware of what may affect the library's operations and image. That is one more reason why regular update meetings with administrators are valuable.

Library Organizational Chart

It is the Director's role to maintain or alter the library organizational chart and reinforce the definition of job responsibilities. The Director inherits an organizational culture, and written expectations in the form of job descriptions and contract language. The ongoing task is to alter these organizational details in order to stay aligned with institutional changes in teaching, learning, discovery, and research.

The staff organizational chart within academic libraries will likely include professional librarians and non-librarian staff, multiple classifications, and perhaps unions or public sector employment regulations. The result is that it is complex to change job duties. Lines can easily develop between people in terms of tasks they will and will not do, or didn't know they were supposed to do. Within the total library staff, there are significant differences in the conditions of employment, and that drives what job changes are realistic, how well such changes will be accepted, and the overall approach to changing job duties.

An administrator's role is to make it clear in daily operations that everyone who works in the library, regardless of job definition, is on the same library team, and that each person's work is necessary to the operation of the whole library. It is so much better if everyone thinks "horizontally" ("We're all on this team") rather than vertically ("My work is more/less important than yours"). How deeply divided the staff is over status and conditions of work will likely determine an administrator's chances of effectively leading the whole staff.

Organize Librarian Roles

There are several ways the Director and librarians can organize the roles of the librarians. A wise Director uses a liaison model, and evaluates other models against the benefits of a liaison model. Liaison librarians know the subject resources, and work with relatively few faculty in that assigned discipline. Hence, the chances are improved that the liaison librarian can provide higher quality and personalized library work with faculty and students. The liaison librarian manages collection development, teaches information literacy, and provides research services. A liaison model brings benefits to departments and political support back to the library. A Director and the librarians should use a liaison model as the norm against which they determine how best to define their work duties.

Think and Act Like an Entrepreneur

The term "entrepreneur" may not be on the Director's job description, but in fact a Director should think and act like an entrepreneur on behalf of the library. Entrepreneurs take initiative, and the Director needs to develop an entrepreneurial culture within the library staff. Passively waiting for students and faculty to use the library for the "right scholarly reasons" is not good enough. Regardless of the size and mission of the institution, the library Director and staff can exhibit an entrepreneurial orientation, and find ways to play offense, generate revenue, promote usage, and in unexpected ways contribute to the institution's academic life.

Think and Act Like a Politician

The Director needs to think and act like a politician in the positive sense of the word "politician." That means building a network of campus connections, planning two and three steps ahead of immediate decisions, and being aware of the short- and longer-term cost of actions. The "Director-as-politician" must pay attention to the images and perceptions of the library held by people in Budget, Facilities, Student Life, and Administration, and be intentional about maintaining or improving those images. The need to think strategically like a politician never ends. The Director can never take for granted the neutral to positive status of the library. The Director must always think in political terms about the position of the library within the institution, the next few steps to take, and the political cost and benefit of actions. See Part I for further discussion on the Director's political role.

Administrative Assistant

The term "Administrative Assistant" connotes that this person is part of the administrative team, even though classified as a staff position. The allegiance needs to be with the Director and the institution's administrative side. The Administrative Assistant doesn't make decisions about the operation of the library, and must be publicly and privately supportive of administrative decisions. The library Administrative Assistant holds a unique role as a staff person with access to information that the rest of the staff does not and should not have (e.g., personnel issues or budget details). Discretion is paramount.

APPLICATION

Introduction

Within days of a new academic library Director starting work, there should be a staff meeting with the Director's supervisor, who should say, in effect, "This is why I hired this person, and these are the priorities." Such an introduction sets the context for the new Director. It makes it clear to everyone that there is a "to do" list. It also indicates that the position of library Director is an institutional position, responsible to the Provost, and not just a library position.

Update Meetings

An academic library administrator should have regularly scheduled individual update meetings with as many librarians as possible for the purpose of communication, building trust, and staying focused on what is of highest importance for the library. It is better to meet often (biweekly) and for a short period of time (half an hour or less). The meetings should be recurring, held in the administrator's office, and rarely skipped. Some librarians (and administrators) may question the use of time for these meetings. However, having update meetings is foundational for a well-managed and effective library, and they are one factor in developing a high level of professionalism throughout the staff. This is where the dual role of leader and manager begins for each administrator.

Entrepreneurial Activities

Administrators should think with staff about ways to promote the use of the library in order to bring enough people in the doors, use the electronic resources on its website, borrow enough of the physical items, and play a visible role in the institution's educational efforts. Spend money on advertising, host events in the library, and use video and social media to get attention. Raising money is part of the Director's job, so work with institutional staff to acquire gifts and endowment funds. Depending on the institution's size and mission, an entrepreneurial academic library might pursue grants, participate in large-scale consortia, be active in data curation projects, or in scholarly publishing projects.

Administrative Assistant Duties

If there is an Administrative Assistant for the library Director, one basic task is coordinating the scheduling of meetings for the upcoming academic year for the Director and staff. Scheduling is best done in mid-summer, well before the Autumn term begins. There is a sequence to setting recurring meetings. First, schedule the academic calendar, holidays, and other known institutional events. Then schedule the update meetings between the Director and Provost. Next, block out any other recurring meetings the Director has, such as with the Deans, other administrators, and professional library meetings. This makes it clearer how to set the dates and reserve the rooms for recurring library meetings (e.g., staff meetings, professional development times, and individual update meetings with direct reports). Scheduling people and meeting places is complex, and the time to do it is before school starts, so that it is set for the academic year.

Tasks done by an Administrative Assistant might include:

- scheduling for the Director, all staff meetings, and for building usage,
- point of contact for maintenance and custodial issues,
- budget, and especially reconciling purchases between the budget and accounting departments,
- planning details for professional development and conferences,
- writing announcements, presentations, and editing documents according to the library Style Guide,
- organizing and maintaining electronic documents used for operation and governance,
- planning social events, and
- other duties depending on the skills, the need, and available time.

READING

STANDARDS AND GUIDELINES

Association of College and Research Libraries. "Standards for Libraries in Higher Education." Chicago: American Library Association, 2011. www.ala.org/acrl/standards/standardslibraries.

ADVICE AND RESEARCH

Alire, Camila A., and G. Edward Evans. *Academic Librarianship*. New York: Neal-Schuman Publishers, Inc., 2010.

Applegate, Rachel. *Managing the Small College Library*. Santa Barbara, CA: Libraries Unlimited, 2010.

Ashkenas, Ron. "More Direct Reports Make Life Easier." Harvard Business Review. HBR Blog Network. http://blogs.hbr.org/2012/09/more-direct-reports -make-life.

Begum, Shakeela. "Fund-Raising and the Academic Library: Generating Internal and External Support." In *The Associate University Librarian Handbook: A Resource Guide*, edited by Bradford Lee Eden. Lanham, MD: Scarecrow Press, 2012.

Berstler, Andrea D. "Running the Library As a Business." In *The Entrepreneurial Librarian: Essays on the Infusion of Private-Business Dynamism into the Professional Service*, edited by Mary Krautter, Mary Beth Lock, and Mary G. Scanlon. Jefferson, NC: McFarland & Company, Inc., 2012.

Bolman, Lee G., and Joan V. Gallos. *Reframing Academic Leadership*. San Francisco: Jossey-Bass, 2011.

Budd, John M. *The Changing Academic Library: Operations, Culture, Environments*, 2nd ed. Chicago: Association of College and Research Libraries, 2012.

Carpenter, Maria Taesil Hudson. "Cheerleader, Opportunity Seeker, and Master Strategist: ARL Directors as Entrepreneurial Leaders." *College & Research Libraries*. 73, no. 1 (January 2012): 11–32.

Drucker, Peter F. "What Makes an Effective Executive." In *HBR's 10 Must Reads on Leadership*. Boston: Harvard Business Review Press, 2011.

Eden, Bradford Lee, ed. *The Associate University Librarian Handbook: A Resource Guide*. Lanham, MD: Scarecrow Press, 2012.

Free Management Library. http://managementhelp.org.

Hernon, Peter, Ronald R. Powell, and Arthur P. Young. "Academic Library Directors: What Do They Do?" *College & Research Libraries* 65, no. 6 (November 2004): 538–563.

Hernon, Peter, Ronald R. Powell, and Arthur P. Young. *The Next Library Leadership: Attributes of Academic and Public Library Directors*. Westport, CT: Libraries Unlimited, 2003.

Hernon, Peter, Ronald R. Powell, and Arthur P. Young. "University Library Directors in the Association of Research Libraries: The Next Generation, Part One." *College & Research Libraries* 62, no. 2 (March 2001): 116–146.

Hernon, Peter, Ronald R. Powell, and Arthur P. Young. "University Library Directors in the Association of Research Libraries: The Next Generation, Part Two." *College & Research Libraries* 63, no. 1 (January 2002): 73–90.

Kearley, Jamie P., and Deborah McCarthy. "Caught in the Middle: Managing Competing Expectations." In *Middle Management in Academic and Public Libraries*, edited by Tom Diamond. Santa Barbara, CA: Libraries Unlimited, 2011: 103–114.

Kotter, John P. "What Leaders Really Do." In *HBR's 10 Must Reads on Leadership*. Boston: Harvard Business Review Press, 2011: 37–55.

Library Leadership & Management Association (LLAMA). A Division of the American Library Association. www.ala.org/llama.

"Marketing @ your library." Chicago: Association of College and Research Libraries. www.ala.org/acrl/issues/marketing.

Matthews, Brian. "Think Like a Startup. A White Paper to Inspire Library Entrepreneurialism." April 2012. http://vtechworks.lib.vt.edu/bitstream/handle/10919/18649/Think%20like%20a%20STARTUP.pdf?sequence=1.

Mosley, Pixey Anne. *Transitioning from Librarian to Middle Manager*. Westport, CT: Libraries Unlimited, 2004.

Phan, T., L. Hardesty, J. Hug, and C. Sheckells. *Academic Libraries: 2012* (NCES 2014-038). Washington, DC: U.S. Department of Education, National Center for Education Statistics, 2014. http://nces.ed.gov/pubsearch.

Soules, Aline. "Balance of Authority and Responsibility in Middle Management." In *Middle Management in Academic and Public Libraries,* edited by Tom Diamond. Santa Barbara, CA: Libraries Unlimited, 2011.

Wayman, Matthew J., Billie E. Walker, and John D. Shank. "The Penn State University Libraries Administrative Leadership Development Program: A Proposal." In *Middle Management in Academic and Public Libraries,* edited by Tom Diamond. Santa Barbara, CA: Libraries Unlimited, 2011.

Wood, Elizabeth J., Rush Miller, and Amy Knapp. *Beyond Survival: Managing Academic Libraries in Transition.* Westport, CT: Libraries Unlimited, 2007.

11
New Hires

Administrators' Roles and Accountability

ASSERTION

The academic library Director is accountable for each newly hired person, and for setting the expectation that each needs attributes that will contribute to emerging roles, and hence to the ongoing success of the library.

COMMENTARY

Director's Accountability

The consequences of each new hire are so important that the academic library Director needs to be involved at some level in the hiring of each person. Hiring decisions have a short-term cost of bringing that person into the library's culture. The cost is in staff time and money for the search, hire, and sometimes moving expenses. There is also a cost to bringing that person into the work culture of the library and of the college or university. A good hire results in someone who fills the position as described, but who also has the right interpersonal skills to be part of the library team, and has an interest in learning new roles as they emerge.

There is a longer-term cost if a good hire wasn't made; namely, mediocre job performance, and an indifferent-to-negative impact on the library's internal culture and work with students and faculty. There is a cost in the efforts of subsequent Directors to work with and around that person. There may also be the difficult decision to terminate that person's employment.

The Director is accountable for setting the hiring conditions because of the ongoing impact of each new hire on the library program. All administrators ought to intentionally learn as much as possible about making hiring decisions. It is helpful to attend workshops on hiring, read the literature on hiring, be on hiring committees for positions other than the library, and talk with people with experience and knowledge about hiring, especially those in Human Resources, and faculty who know about management. Becoming proficient at hiring is a top priority for a library administrator.

Director's Involvement

The level of the Director's involvement in a hiring decision depends on the size of the library staff, its organizational structure, and the willingness and availability of the Director to be involved at some level in the process. The Director should be involved in reviewing the job description, especially if it is time to revise it. The Director of a small- to medium-sized staff should be on each hiring committee for librarians and non-librarian staff. In large libraries, if the Director is not personally on the committee, then for both librarian and non-librarian positions the Director needs to:

- ask the right questions of the committee chair,
- expect a satisfactory explanation for why an applicant was chosen, and
- have a personal interview with the finalist.

The Director must be in agreement with the committee's decision, and that is why a personal interview is important.

The Director should influence the composition of a search committee. A committee is both evaluating and recruiting a candidate. The individuals on the committee need judgment skills in evaluating others, and they need to represent the library well, especially to candidates who have job options.

The Director needs to monitor the progress of the search. The Director and the search committee chair should talk about desirable characteristics in a candidate, review the screening criteria, and review the interview process. The chair should brief the Director on the applications being given serious consideration. If the process veers off in a direction that isn't likely to result in a hire which the Director or the Provost will approve, then the Director should intervene and alter or end the search. An unsuccessful search process will not only waste time and money, but may well bruise the library's reputation.

Human Resources Department

Each campus has a defined hiring process, and the Director must read and understand what it means in practice. It is not wise to "work around" the approved instructions and templates. If the process or screening instruments are altered, then it is prudent to first show those revised documents to someone in the Human Resources department. If the library hiring process is outside of the institutional norm, and subsequently a personnel issue results, then the Director will have to explain why the library process did not follow the stipulated steps and documents.

Trust

The underlying issue in a hiring process is the level of trust between the Director and some existing members of the staff. If there is not transparency about why someone was hired (and another candidate not hired), then trust between the administrator and some staff will be diminished, perhaps for years. That will likely affect other working relationships, including those of the person hired. The Director needs to be involved in the hiring process, or stay closely informed, and make sure that by the end the level of trust between staff and the Director is not damaged. If the Director has cause for concern about hiring someone, then not making that hire is a better option (e.g., time, cost, trust, and reputation) than hiring that individual.

Avoiding Personnel Problems

In many institutions, at the end of the search process the Director brings the name of a candidate to the Provost, who then makes the final hiring decision. It is in the interest of the Director and Provost that each person hired be successful, and, at a minimum, not become a personnel problem. The Provost relies on the Director to have made or monitored the hiring process. The Provost is likely to approve the decision if the Provost has learned to trust the Director's judgment, and if there are plausible reasons why this person was chosen, and no causes for concern. However, if the Director makes one or several poor hires, then the working relationship between the Provost and Director is damaged. Poor judgment in hiring is a serious issue. With several poor hires it is likely that the Director will be politically marginalized.

Job Descriptions

It is valuable to periodically review all employee job descriptions, and the assumptions and comparative data that support the classification of each job. A good time to talk about the job description is during the annual performance review. How a position is classified is correlated at some level with its salary. Reviewing and rewriting job descriptions is good for the employee, and good for clarifying the relationship between the employee and administrator. Inaccurate job descriptions can put a library administrator at risk when there is an issue about job duties or performance.

When there is an open position, the job description must always be reviewed. The current staff doing similar work should be involved in this conversation, and advise on a new or revised job description. This is also the time to evaluate the minimum qualifications, and discuss what is absolutely necessary. One never knows who is "out there." Too many minimum qualifications can screen out someone who might otherwise become a terrific employee. For example, experience working in an academic library may seem like a desirable minimum qualification, but in practice may eliminate potentially good candidates who worked in public or school libraries, and in fact could learn quickly to work in an academic environment.

Compensation

The Director has limited ability to alter salaries and benefits, especially of a new hire. There likely is a defined amount of money in the budget for salary and benefits for that position. Within a set salary range, the Director may be able to determine a salary as a function of the person's experience, education, and the level of that salary relative to what others in the library are paid. Salary ranges are commonly set campus-wide by staff in the Finance office, factoring in variables such as comparable job descriptions, salaries, and the local cost of living indices. It is helpful to work with those who make the formulas and acquire the data to make sure they are correct for all library positions.

The desired candidate may ask for more money than is in the budget line, or than other staff in that category receive. Even if there is flexibility on this point, the administrator ought to work closely with contacts in the Human Resources and Finance offices to not make a long-term mistake. Be clear about the salary package with a candidate early in the process so that each side knows if this job is worth pursuing. The administrator doesn't want to get to the end of an expensive hiring process and get locked into a salary negotiation in which the library budget cannot (or the administrator will not) pay what the applicant is asking. At that point, having learned something about the applicant that wasn't evident before, it may be time to say "No thanks. Let's go on to the next person." It may not be worthwhile politically to go to the Provost and ask for additional salary. There may also be subsequent issues among existing staff if a new employee is paid more than the understood salary range.

Office Conditions

If a candidate has job options, then that person will evaluate a job and include cursory perceptions of who the people are who work in this library, the salary and benefits, and the alignment of this institution with the candidate's self-understanding. The physical condition of the library is also a plus or minus when recruiting.

A candidate with job options is going to also evaluate the working conditions, and that usually includes the office space. There are often two considerations:

- the condition of the office, ranging from location, size, noise level, natural lighting, and aesthetics, and
- the expectation for using the office.

It is normal for an administrator to expect that a librarian will be in the building according to a schedule. If the librarian thinks that working from home is the same as working from the library office, then that needs to be clarified during the hiring process. Office space is chronically in short supply in libraries. When an administrator assigns an office to a librarian, then the expectation is for the person to use that office. Working from home should occur under well-defined circumstances, and as a result of a signed memorandum between the Director and librarian.

Always Recruiting

A search committee is simultaneously evaluating and recruiting an applicant. What the applicant knows of the institution, the library, and the job is largely determined by interactions with the administrator and the committee. That is why it is so important to choose committee members who can recruit. Spend time as a committee being clear about the "talking points," and how to answer anticipated questions. What is said by committee members, and how the process unfolds will either encourage an applicant or raise doubts. Doubts might cause that person to either say "no thanks," or to accept the job but with private reservations. Impressions from the hiring process can last a long time and have consequences.

Knowledge of Applicant

It is most desirable to talk with someone who has worked with the applicant, and who is willing to tell the truth about that applicant's work ethic, collegiality, personality, emotional maturity, and character. Those characteristics are the hardest to ascertain in the hiring process, and when a candidate has been misjudged in any of those areas, there will be a price to pay with the staff and maybe for a long time. In a formal or informal conversation about a prospective employee, hope that a reference will tell the truth about the applicant. It isn't always in the self-interest of a supervisor to answer questions honestly, and sometimes there are topics which cannot be discussed. When someone does, be grateful.

Diversity

The Director needs to periodically have an honest conversation with the Provost in order to know the implicit and explicit expectations about the composition of the library staff in terms of diversity. The context of the institution will shape the efforts of diversity in hiring. In turn, the Director will need to make those expectations clear to the search committee. If candidates with certain characteristics are desired, then be clear in your conversations with the search committee.

Questions of diversity in all of its manifestations are linked to who the Director is personally, and the kind of workplace the Director and other administrators desire to develop. Be very clear personally about the characteristics of the people who should work in the library. An administrator also needs to understand the influence he or she has in order to make the library into a successful workplace. That requires some self-knowledge, judgment, and skill at managing the hiring process.

APPLICATION

Interview Process

The defined and customary interview process for an institution is what should be followed when hiring professional or non-professional library employees. A two-day interview for a librarian position is desirable. In addition to formal times with library staff, the person should be interviewed by faculty from relevant academic disciplines. The candidate should present or teach a class, or at least provide a video. Informal times, including meals, are useful for the committee and other library staff to get a better sense of this person. The key is to schedule the time fully, prepare questions for each group, have multiple people watch or talk with the candidate, and then collect evaluations promptly.

Interview Questions

One good way to write interview questions is to look at the job description, and another library document like a strategic plan, and from those documents define the desirable high-level themes for a new hire. Citing places in these documents that support a theme moves the process beyond generic questions. Within each theme formulate one or several questions which hopefully will get the applicant to talk about that theme. The other helpful part is to identify some "Look For" words and phrases to listen for from the applicant. By doing this ahead of time, committee members should better understand desirable characteristics and the meaning of terms. This is also the time to clarify for committee members what should not be talked about, either in a formal interview or in informal settings. Working with the institution's Human Resources guidelines for interviews, give advice to all who are scheduled to interact with a candidate about what is appropriate and not appropriate in conversation. The interview is a time to let the applicant talk, so that committee members can listen for what is said, not said, and how it is said.

Writing

Does it matter if a member of the library staff can write well, or not? If the person is a librarian, then the answer is that it matters considerably in an academic context. Most faculty care about the use of written language, and expect that all who are faculty write at a certain level of proficiency. Mistakes of grammar, syntax, structure, and content reflect back on the library. When hiring a librarian, the ability to write at a level expected of faculty should be one factor in the decision. About the only way to tell if a finalist can write is to read statements on application forms, read any papers listed on a curriculum vita, and check social media sites. If there are doubts, then factor that into the decision. Once hired, an employee's writing skill may not improve, unless that is part of professional development.

Additional Compensation

In addition to a salary and benefits, how else may an employee be compensated? Check with other deans, the Provost, and someone in the Human Resources office to see what others are doing on campus. Some might have funds for merit pay, and use that according to some criteria. There may be a way to provide funds for travel and conferences, especially beyond the amount normally allocated. Staff who use smartphones for work might be compensated for the monthly charges. Library staff with extra duties could receive a stipend for that task. Time and financial support might be negotiated for obtaining another graduate degree. At some institutions, librarians have nine-month contracts for the academic year, similar to those of teaching faculty. These examples indicate to a candidate that the academic library Director is willing and able to improve compensation.

Annual Leave

One area that is sometimes an issue for a prospective hire is annual leave. Especially for staff positions, the number of days of annual leave may seem too low. The person would prefer more time off to compensate for the salary level. While an administrator cannot arbitrarily change annual leave, there might be some options, which would also benefit others on the staff. For example, there are a number of colleges with no summer session (or enrollment is small), and the use of the library is very light. Often, use of the library is low between the end of summer session and the start of the Autumn term. Does the library need to be staffed at its normal levels during the slowest times of the year? Probably not, and perhaps there are ways to grant additional annual leave during slow times. If salaries are low, and not likely to improve much, then annual leave is a variable which the Director might be able to increase, and that would help with hiring and retention.

Hiring a Non-Citizen

There are additional costs if the library hires someone who is not a citizen of the United States. It is wise to be clear with the Provost, the Human Resources department, and the candidate before hiring him or her about who will pay for current and future costs of working in the United States. Will the institution pay for the work card (H-1B visa or green card)? Will the institution pay for attorney fees, which can be significant? These questions must be raised and resolved before a person is hired and moves.

Announcing a New Hire

Except in small-staff libraries, the rest of the library staff are unlikely to know much during the search process. The Director should send periodic e-mails at milestones, but otherwise respect the confidentiality of the process. Hence, it matters how a finalist is introduced, and especially how the newly hired person is introduced. An e-mail and an announcement at a staff meeting are desirable. What the staff need to hear is why this person was hired, and what attributes this person brings that are desirable. On the first day or two, the Director should walk around the library with a new librarian and introduce him or her. Indeed, some introductions to faculty are helpful, including an introduction at departmental faculty meetings. In a number of ways, the Director can set the context for a new person, and should.

READING

STANDARDS AND GUIDELINES

Association of College and Research Libraries. "Standards for Libraries in Higher Education." Chicago: American Library Association, 2011. www.ala.org/acrl/standards/standardslibraries.

"Diversity Standards: Cultural Competency for Academic Libraries (2012)." Chicago: Association of College and Research Libraries, 2012. www.ala.org/acrl/standards/diversity.

"A Guideline for the Screening and Appointment of Academic Librarians Using a Search Committee." Chicago: Association of College and Research Libraries. www.ala.org/acrl/standards/screenapguide.

"A Guideline on Collective Bargaining." Chicago: Association of College and Research Libraries, 2008. www.ala.org/acrl/standards/guidelinecollective.

ADVICE AND RESEARCH

"ACRL Works With CUPA-HR (College and University Professional Association for Human Resources) to Update Academic Library Position Descriptions." Chicago: Association of College and Research Libraries, 2006. www.ala.org/acrl/proftools/personnel/detail#charge.

Alire, Camila A., and G. Edward Evans. *Academic Librarianship.* New York: Neal-Schuman Publishers, Inc., 2010.

Alire, Camila A. "Diversity and Leadership." In *Making a Difference: Leadership and Academic Libraries.* Westport, CT: Libraries Unlimited, 2007.

Applegate, Rachel. *Managing the Small College Library.* Santa Barbara, CA: Libraries Unlimited, 2010.

Giesecke, Joan, and Beth McNeil. *Fundamentals of Library Supervision.* Chicago: American Library Association, 2005.

Hiring and Keeping the Best People. Boston: Harvard Business School Press, 2002.

Neely, Teresa Y., and Lorna Peterson. "Achieving Racial and Ethnic Diversity among Academic and Research Librarians. The Recruitment, Retention, and Advancement of Librarians of Color—A White Paper." *College & Research Libraries News.* October 2007. http://crln.acrl.org/content/68/9/562.full.pdf.

Palo, Eric E., and Kathy L. Peterson. "Human Resources Functions in the Two-Year College Library." In *It's All About Student Learning. Managing Community and Other College Libraries in the 21st Century,* edited by David R. Dowell and Gerard B. McCabe. Westport, CT: Libraries Unlimited, 2006.

Simmons-Welburn, Janice, and Beth McNeil, eds. *Human Resource Management in Today's Academic Library: Meeting Challenges and Creating Opportunities.* Westport, CT: Libraries Unlimited, 2004.

Walter, Scott, and Karen Williams, eds. *The Expert Library: Staffing, Sustaining, and Advancing the Academic Library in the 21st Century.* Chicago: American Library Association, 2010.

12
Priorities

Aligning Work with Library Needs

ASSERTION

An academic library administrator establishes and monitors the expectation that individuals spend their work time on tasks that align with the written priorities of the library.

COMMENTARY

Strategic Plan and Work Plan

Academic library administrators are responsible for the use of time by all library staff. A strategic plan should guide the conversation with a librarian about what work is a priority, in what sequence, over how much time, and what tasks have low or no priority. A "work plan" document describes how the work of an individual for the upcoming academic year fits into the library's strategic plan. It also sets the context for regularly scheduled update meetings between the librarian and the administrator, the end-of-year evaluation, and (if applicable) the faculty evaluation process for promotion and tenure. This work plan is also the place to outline professional development, including both upcoming and longer-term goals.

Establish Priorities

Each administrator needs to make sure that the library priorities are established, clear to everyone, and indeed guide what people actually do with their work time. When a staff member says he or she is "too busy," then a library administrator needs to look at what that person is doing relative to the library priorities. There may be too many priorities, or some may take too much time. The administrator and librarian should talk about dropping or deferring some tasks of low priority. Indeed, an administrator needs to examine his or her workload in the same way.

It is easy for librarians to spend work time on projects that interest them, but are of minimal value to the library's written priorities. By contrast, classroom faculty may commonly study, research, and teach what interests them. Librarians, however, work in an organization that functions better when there are defined goals and tasks, and individuals work on their part of those goals. Part of each administrator's job is to translate those library-wide goals into specific tasks or projects. These high-priority tasks need to actually get done, while other tasks can go lower on the "to do" list. The projects of value need to be clear in each librarian's annual work plan (which can be revised during the year) and discussed in update meetings.

A Few Priorities

The Director can have the staff working on too many initiatives at once. Each administrator is the keeper of the overall work priority list, its sequence, and timeline. Individuals become weary when everything is of "importance" and the list is too long. If there are more than a few priorities, then the quality of work suffers. Eventually, everyone understands that all these tasks can't possibly be of equal importance.

APPLICATION

Seeing the Strategic Plan

The entire strategic plan needs to be seen in various places and times. It should be on the library intranet. Parts of it should be on an individual librarian's written work plan. It could be summarized on a poster and displayed. It needs to be shared with the Provost. Academic library administrators need to refer to specific parts of it, and be the keepers of its vision. Work tasks need a context, and administrators and staff need to remind each other that each task is derived from an agreed-upon plan.

Defining Core Competencies

The strategic plan will define work priorities, and that will make it clear that some tasks can be dropped. The administrative challenge is to align existing staff, their skills, and what they do during the workday with what currently needs to be done in the library. When viewed this way, a short list of core competencies can be developed. A review of procedures and work flow in each department will show what skills everyone needs. These "core competencies" then show omissions in job descriptions, and point to needs for professional development.

READING

STANDARDS AND GUIDELINES

Association of College and Research Libraries. "Standards for Libraries in Higher Education." Chicago: American Library Association, 2011. www.ala.org/acrl/standards/standardslibraries.

ADVICE AND RESEARCH

Smith, Dennis J., Jessi Hurd, and LeEtta Schmidt. "Developing Core Competencies for Library Staff. How University of South Florida Library Re-evaluated Its Workforce." *College & Research Library News* 74, no. 1 (2013): 14–35.

13
Professional Development

Investing in All Staff

ASSERTION

An academic library administrator allocates budget and time for all library staff to learn how to work, how to work together, and how to continually learn new skills and content.

COMMENTARY

Reliable Way to Improve

Investing time and money in the professional development of each staff member, and making ongoing professional development a priority, is a reliable way to improve:

- individual work performance,
- staff morale, and
- the status of the library on campus.

Making professional development a priority changes the library culture. It takes time, money, and alignment with the library's mission, goals, and strategic plan. Investing in professional development for all sends a valuable message: "All who work in this library are on the same team. Everyone's work is important in order for the library to be effective at a high level. The library needs the knowledge and skills of each person to be as good as possible. Therefore, the library is going to invest in each one of you."

Teaching How to Work

Not every employee has learned how to work at an expected level. An individual may not have experience working at the level of a professional in an academic community. An individual may not know how to prioritize time, divide a large project into incremental steps, or judge the level of detail appropriate for the task. An academic library administrator needs to help calibrate the norms of quality and time for various types of work. Setting norms and teaching each staff member how to work and at what level of quality is basic to building a team.

Teaching About the Job

Not everyone knows how to do a job the "right way," or at the level expected by influential faculty. An administrator needs to work with each new hire during the first year to be sure that the person knows the expected scope and level of performance. This deals with the specifics of what it means to be a "professional" in this institution and in this library. It ranges widely, from attendance, attitude, customer service, and interpersonal relations to the expected level of appearance. Some of this is best done by following standards set by the leaders within the library and some of it in update meetings. A mentoring program with an assigned mentor is very helpful.

How to Work Together

Within an academic library the employees have very different levels of status, mirroring the academic context of the library. The librarians have professional graduate degrees, and are usually aligned with the faculty. Others are classified as staff. Some are in unions. The administrative task is to set the expectation that all are on the same "library team," and really do need to work together. If the cliques are aligned along job titles, then the administrator needs to intentionally work with all staff on how to work together.

Individual's Trajectory

One purpose of professional development is to help each individual identify the direction for his or her professional life, and determine if that trajectory aligns with the needs of the library. The library should invest in an employee's training, but there is no obligation to invest time and money in everything the employee wants to do. The academic library Director needs to decide if the result of that professional development is in some way related to what the library really needs (or will need).

Professional development occurs in multiple areas:

- how to work,
- how to work together,
- learning new skills,
- keeping up with the content in one's academic area, and
- obtaining an additional degree.

Librarians need to keep up with how vendors and organizations package content, and in general with developments in their academic disciplines. That means reading journals, reviews, blogs, and attending conferences. It may also mean doing scholarly research on some aspect of librarianship at a level capable of publication. Or, some librarians might go back to school for an advanced degree in a content area.

Director's Professional Development

The Director needs to invest in his or her own professional development, but also be protective of the time it takes to administer a library. There are too many opportunities. A judgment about the value of conference attendance must factor in cost, time away, and a connection to the library's strategic plan. It is desirable to participate in activities of the Association of College and Research Libraries, or a similar regional professional group.

The investment of time and money in an administrator's professional development is related to where the library should be in a few years, and what the administrator needs to lead it. The institution will often pay for these opportunities, or for the cost of being gone. An administrator needs to connect the dots between the institution's money, the administrator's time, and the value to the library. This is especially true if another graduate degree is involved.

Student Employees

Except in small libraries, the Director is not likely to be involved in hiring, training, and managing student workers. However, the Director needs to monitor what the supervisors of these student workers do in establishing hiring criteria, training materials, work expectations, and management procedures. Many students have not had much prior work experience, or the kind of work experience that values customer service at a high level. Library-using students and faculty often interact with student workers before interacting with regular staff. Hiring, training, and managing student workers is important because of the influence student workers have when interacting with faculty and students.

APPLICATION

When?

How can an academic library administrator encourage professional development and find time for it without having a negative impact on the operation of the library during an academic term? This is a question which should be talked about with the staff. When days and times are agreed upon, then times should be scheduled for the upcoming academic year. For example, a retreat might occur sometime during the several weeks prior to the start of Autumn term. A retreat can be in the library so the building stays open, is staffed with student workers, but the regular staff is just steps away if needed. Often academic departments have retreats prior to the start of the academic year, so holding a library retreat before departmental retreats allows librarians to attend both.

Webinars (and the technology enabling online meetings) have transformed how and when much professional development occurs. They not only save the cost of travel, but can often be viewed at different times of day. Administrators and staff can participate in a webinar during the workday and in the library. That is high-quality and cost-efficient professional development. Or, video conferencing can be used to discuss topics with regional or national colleagues.

Reading websites, blogs, RSS feeds, and online journals will likely occur during the time set aside for reading e-mails, like early in the morning. Professional reading will also occur at all kinds of odd moments during the day on a smartphone or tablet. And there are always evenings and weekends for professional reading.

Reporting Back

All completed professional development experiences should be recorded on a document on the library intranet. In addition to keeping a record of who did what, and a phrase about what was learned, the academic library Director needs to establish appropriate ways for individuals to share what was learned. A written report can be linked from the document on the intranet. Informal sharing can occur during scheduled brown bag lunch times, or during staff meetings.

Teaching Students How to Work

It is best to have the training instructions and videos for each student job posted on the library intranet. Train each student and track that each module of the training occurred. The more things are written, shown in photos and videos, and easily available, then the better for ongoing relearning. Short videos and web-based tutorials are helpful. Write down the expectations, show examples with video, photographs, and diagrams, and then monitor how the student is doing. Investing time in training each new student is worth the cost of a staff member's time.

Customer Service

Teach the same customer service skills to students and library staff. Write what they need to know and do. Make videos and web tutorials showing examples. Be clear about desirable communication skills, and then provide professional development on learning those skills. The Student Services or Human Resources departments may have already contracted for this training, and the library staff should be in on this same training. Perhaps the campus police office has a person who can do a workshop for all library staff on handling difficult patrons. Usually all employees are taught about confidentiality when hired, but it is good to reinforce that in the library context.

Teaching Staff How to Work

Teaching staff how to be professionals and work at a high level can occur in several ways. One is for an administrator to do this internally with a staff workshop. Another way is to hire a consultant to do a workshop. Sometimes job shadowing at another academic library can be helpful. If going to another library is not feasible, then video conferencing with someone at another library is an efficient alternative. The real teaching is in the ongoing modeling and conversation between supervisors and staff. Administrators need to keep "how to work" as a topic of conversation.

New Employee Orientation

Professional development begins with teaching each new employee how to get things done in the library. The information that everyone should know needs to be listed in a chart (e.g., a topic, where written directions are stored on the library intranet for that topic, as well as the name of the person in charge of that topic). A new employee needs to work through this chart, checking off the topics as learned. It is helpful to assign someone to guide the new employee through this process. Expect that person to cover an orientation curriculum of more than just the routine tasks. The new person needs to learn the culture of the library, and how tasks are done in this institution. It is an administrator's business to see that this orientation is established and implemented. Create the curriculum for new employees, and perhaps pay a stipend to someone who orients the new person during the first three or six months.

Coaching and Mentoring

There are times when it is helpful to establish a relationship of mentoring or coaching for certain employees. There is plenty of material on coaching and mentoring, and the Director ought to read some and seek advice before starting. The definition or model of coaching and mentoring is not nearly as important as actually being a recipient of coaching or mentoring.

Coaching can be done by an administrator working with a librarian, or it can be done by someone external to the library, in the model of an "executive coach." Time and money are invested in coaching because either the individual's work performance would likely benefit from coaching, or the coaching is viewed as high-quality personal professional development for an administrator. The coaching is about developing judgment, using best practices, and making good decisions. If a library Director has a coach, it is more likely to be an external coach, hired by a Provost as an investment.

Cross-Train

It is wise to define what tasks need a backup person. Well-prepared libraries cross-train for tasks which can't be temporarily shut down when the person who normally does that job is absent. The library looks inept if a service expected by patrons is unavailable because someone is absent from work. Post the chart on the intranet. Write down the steps for doing these tasks. Train someone just well enough to follow the instructions, do the basics, and keep the task going.

Inexpensive Professional Development

Effective professional development does not always require a budget. Some can be simple and inexpensive, done without travel, without fees, and during times when school is not in session:

- Peer coaching and mentoring within the library staff
- Brown bag lunch-time discussions of articles or professional development

- Webinars
- Video conferencing
- Experts from campus departments presenting at staff meetings: for example, Information Technology, campus safety, or faculty who know the research about teaching, marketing, customer service, website design, or library interior design
- Staff-presented skill building
- In-house retreats
- In-house blogs on specific topics
- Videos showing practices from another academic library

The key is to find time to prepare, and time to do these things with some or all of the staff.

Professional Associations

All academic librarians should belong to the American Library Association's academic division, the Association of College and Research Libraries. Those membership dues should be paid from the academic institution's funds. There are also subject-specific groups, and where appropriate librarians ought to belong and participate. For the Director, professional networking is so valuable. It can occur locally and regionally, informally or more formally through a consortium, or it can occur through connections made through national groupings of directors.

Research, Writing, and Publication

If librarians have faculty rank, and if research, writing, and publication are part of the evaluation criteria for promotion, then an administrator needs to develop consensus among librarians about when it is appropriate to do research and write, and the impact of the time it takes to do these activities on their other duties. If working with faculty and students during the term is the highest priority, then a librarian's own research and writing should occur during summer, or when time is defined (e.g., leave, sabbatical, or grant) and that FTE is backfilled by another person. However it is done, and especially if the top priority is working with faculty and students during a term, then the librarian and an administrator need to be clear about an acceptable use of time for research and writing.

Additional Degree

When an employee returns to school for an additional degree while working in the library, should the administrator make any accommodations? First, find out if the institution has any policies about working full time and attending school. Sometimes the employee really can work full time and take a class, with an acceptably small impact on job performance. If the coursework has an impact on job performance, then the administrator and the employee should write an agreement (with the help of someone in Human Resources) by which the employee temporarily reduces FTE. The administrator should be careful to neither make an agreement counter to the institution's policy, nor set a disruptive precedent among library staff, such as asking other staff to cover for the employee who has returned to school. Supporting a return to school is desirable, but there is likely an impact on job performance and on setting a precedent.

Administrator's Research and Writing

It is a rare library Director who can work in an all-consuming administrative position and still research and write at a level capable of publication, and in the process not harm the operation of the library. It is very hard to squeeze time from the normal administrative routine, leaving the options of either a defined leave, or letting go of research and writing. To research, write, and publish realistically requires time without administrative duties. That usually means a leave, a sabbatical, or grant money to buy out some weeks, and pay someone else to backfill duties. Limited writing perhaps can be done during the summer, although summer is usually prime time for preparation for the upcoming year.

Administrator's Daily Reading

There are dozens of websites, blogs, and RSS and Twitter feeds that an administrator could read. At minimum, and if time is justified, an academic library administrator should check:

Chronicle of Higher Education
   http://chronicle.com/section/Home/5

ACRL Insider Weblog
   www.acrl.ala.org/acrlinsider

ACRLog
   http://acrlog.org

ACRL Twitter
   @ALA_ACRL

Library Leadership & Management Association
   www.ala.org/llama

Library Leadership & Management
   http://journals.tdl.org/llm1/index

College & Research Libraries News
http://crln.acrl.org

College & Research Libraries
http://crl.acrl.org

Checklists

It is smart to develop checklists for a wide variety of library procedures, and for the training which goes with each. These checklists should be available on an intranet for learning and doing tasks ranging from routine to highly specialized. The use of checklists should significantly reduce errors ("I forgot"), excuses ("But I thought . . ."), and lead to a predictably better-operated library. They are also invaluable when someone is absent, and someone else needs to fill in.

READING

STANDARDS AND GUIDELINES

Arch, Xan, Jennifer Falkowski, Liladhar Pendse, and Emily Symonds. "Orienting and Educating New Librarians about Privacy Obligations: Guidelines for Administrators." Chicago: American Library Association, 2009. www.ala .org/llama/sites/ala.org.llama/files/content/publications/orienting_and _educat.pdf.

Association of College and Research Libraries. "Standards for Libraries in Higher Education." Chicago: American Library Association, 2011. www.ala.org/acrl/ standards/standardslibraries.

Association of College and Research Libraries. "Statement on Professional Development." Chicago: Association of College and Research Libraries, 2000. www.ala.org/acrl/publications/whitepapers/acrlstatement.

ADVICE AND RESEARCH

ALA Connect. "Mentoring." http://connect.ala.org/mentorconnect-help.

Alire, Camila A., and G. Edward Evans. *Academic Librarianship.* New York: Neal-Schuman Publishers, Inc., 2010.

Applegate, Rachel. *Managing the Small College Library.* Santa Barbara, CA: Libraries Unlimited, 2010.

Coaching and Mentoring. How to Develop Top Talent and Achieve Stronger Performance. Boston: Harvard Business Review Press, 2004.

Edwards, Phillip M., Elaine Z. Jennerich, and Jennifer L. Ward. "Supporting a Culture of Library Research at the University of Washington at Seattle." In *An Introduction to Staff Development in Academic Libraries,* edited by Elizabeth Connor. New York: Routledge, 2009.

Ekart, Donna F., Jennifer Heikkila Furrey, and Ellen R. Urton. "Welcome! Creating an Effective New Employee Orientation Program at Kansas State Libraries." In *An Introduction to Staff Development in Academic Libraries,* edited by Elizabeth Connor. New York: Routledge, 2009.

Gawande, Atul. *The Checklist Manifesto. How to Get Things Right.* New York: Henry Holt, 2009.

Giesecke, Joan and Beth McNeil. *Fundamentals of Library Supervision.* Chicago: American Library Association, 2005.

Hiring and Keeping the Best People. Boston: Harvard Business Review Press, 2002.

Hollister, Christopher V. *Handbook of Academic Writing for Librarians.* Chicago: Association of College and Research Libraries, 2013.

Krautter, Mary, and Christine Fischer. "Working Together: Public and Technical Services Perspectives." In *Middle Management in Academic and Public Libraries,* edited by Tom Diamond. Santa Barbara, CA: Libraries Unlimited, 2011.

Levine, Jenny. "Mentoring FAQ." ALA Connect. Chicago: American Library Association, 2009. http://connect.ala.org/mentorconnect-help.

"Mentoring Program." Chicago: American Library Association. Library Leadership & Management Association (LLAMA). www.ala.org/llama/llama-mentoring -program.

Rubin, Rhea Joyce. *Defusing the Angry Patron. A How-To-Do-It Manual for Librarians and Paraprofessionals,* 2nd ed. New York: Neal-Schuman Publishers, Inc., 2010.

Smallwood, Carol, and Rebecca Tolley-Stokes. *Mentoring in Librarianship: Essays on Working with Adults and Students to Further the Profession.* Jefferson, NC: McFarland & Company, 2012.

Stanley, John. "Improving Communications Skills." In *It's All About Student Learning. Managing Community and Other College Libraries in the 21st Century,* edited by David R. Dowell and Gerard B. McCabe. Westport, CT: Libraries Unlimited, 2006.

Ting, Sharon, and Peter Seisco, eds. *CCL Handbook of Coaching. A Guide for the Leader Coach.* San Francisco: Jossey-Bass, 2006.

Trotta, Marcia. *Staff Development on a Shoestring.* New York: Neal-Schuman Publishers, Inc., 2011.

Willis, Mark R. *Dealing with Difficult People in the Library.* Chicago: American Library Association, 1999.

14
Accountability

Monitoring and Evaluating Work

ASSERTION

The academic library Director is accountable for the establishment and implementation of procedures and timelines to monitor and evaluate the quality of work done by all library staff.

COMMENTARY

Work Plan

A work plan is a written statement of what an academic librarian or administrator intends to do during an upcoming year, all within the context of the library's mission statement, goals, and strategic plan. It is important to see those guiding words when outlining what someone intends to do, is doing, or has done. The plan may include information from the previous year, or from a faculty evaluation.

Where librarians are faculty, the organization of the work plan document should align with the categories upon which faculty are evaluated. This work plan is the basis for conversation during update meetings about the librarian's work, the end-of-year annual review, and the longer-term professional development plan.

Annual Review

The academic library Director needs to make sure that librarians make a work plan by the agreed-upon date, use it during the year in update meetings when discussing work, and then use it as the basis for an annual review with an administrator. What is said and written during the annual review should not be a surprise. The annual review should be a summary of what the employee has done, and how well that work was done, all of which should have been discussed in update meetings during the year. What is important is that some kind of annual review occurs, is written, and is on file.

Pre-Tenure Review

It is highly desirable that librarians have a performance review similar to the pre-tenure review done for teaching faculty. This usually occurs at the end of the third year of employment. It commonly includes evaluation from librarians, the Director, and faculty. This is the formal occasion for a review of a librarian's work and suitability for retention as part of the faculty.

Outstanding Librarians

It is expensive to go through the process of hiring a new librarian. In addition to time and money, there can be additional costs, such as regret from those who miss the previous person, or who wanted another candidate hired. Consequently, when a newly hired librarian turns out to be valuable, then it is smart for multiple reasons to keep that person engaged in satisfying work, and not open to offers of employment elsewhere. Even in large libraries, if one or more notable librarians leave, then the faculty perception is that the library lost quality and status. Real or perceived contagion may create doubt about working there. That is disruptive from the standpoint of other library staff, and from those faculty members who valued that librarian. If there is a pattern of losing well-liked and outstanding librarians, then that may reflect poorly on either the Director's management, or (if the issues are fiscal) institutional priorities.

The Director needs to understand what motivates exemplary librarians and why they would like to stay. Conversely, what are the irritants that are strong enough to make them look elsewhere? Is there anything the Director can do to reduce or eliminate these barriers to job satisfaction? The Director needs to have private talks with the Provost about proactive measures to keep key employees from leaving easily when job offers come to them.

Unsatisfactory Work

One point of having biweekly meetings with key employees is to monitor how each person's work is going. If the Director is hearing complaints about a staff member, or observes work issues, then the Director needs to determine the validity and seriousness of those observations. This is best done individually and quietly. If the Director does not act, then that can undermine staff morale, be perceived as weakness, lead to criticism of the Director's leadership, and result in some staff saying or doing things they might regret. The biweekly update meeting gives clues about an employee's job performance, and provides an opportunity to deal with that situation.

Annual Review of Director

The Director may want to have the librarians, or the whole library staff, evaluate the Director's work performance at the end of an academic year. It is common for administrators to evaluate the work of others, but it may not be common for the entire staff to evaluate the Director's work. Such an evaluation is best done through an evaluation instrument that outlines the Director's work expectations, and then invites comments. Having the staff evaluate the Director means that the Director really wants to know what the staff think. Being evaluated may be very good for the Director's image as an administrator, as it shows that he or she is not above being evaluated by the people being led. An evaluation may also bruise the Director's ego and uncover surprising perceptions.

APPLICATION

Update Meetings

The purpose of an update meeting is communication about what the librarian is doing, how well the work is going, upcoming tasks and events, and if the librarian might need additional resources or political intervention. While an update meeting with a direct report is often thought about in terms of "control," a much better way to understand these meetings is in terms of communication, trust, and affirmation of good work. The librarian needs to know that the academic library administrator knows about the librarian's work, cares about the librarian's well-being, and that work well done is noted.

When a task is completed, then that becomes part of what is reviewed in an annual evaluation. Items in these update meetings roll up into an annual summary of what was accomplished. There should be no surprises in what an administrator says or writes in an annual review. Judgments about the quality and effectiveness of work should have already been discussed throughout the year. Update meetings keep staff and tasks on track, and provide a record of what was accomplished, as well as being ongoing occasions for talking about effectiveness.

READING

STANDARDS AND GUIDELINES

Association of College and Research Libraries. "Standards for Libraries in Higher Education." Chicago: American Library Association, 2011. www.ala.org/acrl/standards/standardslibraries.

ADVICE AND RESEARCH

Alire, Camila A., and G. Edward Evans. *Academic Librarianship*. New York: Neal-Schuman Publishers, Inc., 2010.

Ancona, Deborah, Thomas W. Malone, Wanda J. Orlikowski, and Peter M. Senge. "In Praise of the Incomplete Leader." In *HBR's 10 Must Reads on Leadership*. Boston: Harvard Business Review Press, 2011.

Applegate, Rachel. *Managing the Small College Library*. Santa Barbara, CA: Libraries Unlimited, 2010.

Ashkenas, Ron. "More Direct Reports Make Life Easier." *Harvard Business Review*. HBR Blog Network. http://blogs.hbr.org/2012/09/more-direct-reports -make-life.

Brown, Phillipa, and M. Sue Baughman. *Conversations that Work: Conducting Performance Assessments* (ACRL Active Guide #3). Chicago: Association of College and Research Libraries, 2010.

Harvard Business Review on Appraising Employee Performance. Boston: Harvard Business Press, 2005.

Hiring and Keeping the Best People. Boston: Harvard Business School Press, 2002.

Martin, Jason. "Symbols, Sagas, Rites, and Rituals. An Overview of Organizational Culture in Libraries." *College & Research Libraries News* 73, no. 6 (June 2012): 348–349.

McNeil, Beth. "Managing Work Performance and Career Development" in *Human Resource Management in Today's Academic Library*, edited by Janice Simmons-Welburn and Beth McNeil. Westport, CT: Libraries Unlimited, 2004.

Watkins, Michael. *The First 90 Days: Critical Success Strategies for New Leaders at All Levels*. Boston: Harvard Business Review Press, 2003.

15
Decision-Making

Processes for Library Governance

ASSERTION

The academic library Director defines the processes by which decisions are made within the library, by whom, for what topics, and enforces the use of those processes.

COMMENTARY

Inherited Norms for Decision-Making

If meeting staff is the first priority when the academic library Director is new, then right behind is learning the inherited decision-making process. How is the staff accustomed to decision-making, what decisions, and by whom? The Director needs to know this from the first few days, follow that process, and enforce its use. It is understandable if he or she sees something annoying, and wants to make a decisive statement by removing or changing it. However, to not follow the existing process and instead unilaterally remove signs, reassign office space, add or subtract a job duty, or reallocate a budget line, all raise underlying questions of process. Until the Director understands the process by which decisions have been made, then it is smarter in the long term to keep a list of all the things, procedures, or attitudes seen or heard in the library which initially caused one to wince. Do not inadvertently get off to a bad start with one or several employees by making a decision which is either viewed as wrong, or as having been made with the wrong process.

Decision-Making Process

It is the Director's prerogative to define who is involved in making what kind of decisions. It is important to be clear that some decisions are the Director's business and some are collaborative. Clarity provides accountability. Not everything is everybody's business. Especially in a small library, the Director should be clear about the process for making decisions. When staff work side-by-side and everyone knows each other, then it is easy to make decisions based on who is asking, and make decisions too quickly. When someone asks "Have a minute?" then the Director should be careful what is said in that unscheduled meeting. Resist making decisions without going through the agreed-upon process. Unintended consequences of decisions made outside of the process will make the Director appear administratively inept.

Management Team

In a library with under ten employees, decisions can be made by the Director and everyone else in a staff meeting. With a few more employees, the Director should meet individually as well as with the group of librarians.

In a large library with several administrators, the Director and those other administrators are the management team. The Director's job is to bring this group together in order to act on a shared set of values and assumptions. If one or several administrators are really not in agreement about the library's direction, or if some believe that their success comes at the expense of another's failure, then the Director either needs to change attitudes or managers.

Update Meetings for Governance

Recurring update meetings between an administrator and a librarian are basic for communicating about work, but they are equally basic for the governance of the library. The conversations go two ways in private. Ideally, the Director and a librarian can develop and sustain a working relationship of mutual trust and respect. These update meetings are important for exchanging differing perspectives. Things can be said which are less likely to be said in staff meetings, which can be unproductive because some people talk too much, others too little, and not everybody is interested in everything on the agenda.

Internal Committees

Academic library administrators and the Administrative Assistant should do as many of the background tasks as possible so that librarians and frontline staff spend most of their time on the library needs of faculty and students. While a few standing committees are necessary, administrators should monitor the need and frequency of meetings, and reduce them when the price is too high in terms of staff time measured against results. Periodically ask how many salary dollars are expended during this meeting, and if something of higher value could have been done instead. Sometimes ad hoc committees are more useful because they go out of existence when a task is finished.

APPLICATION

Staff Meetings

It is the academic library Director's role to convene staff meetings and influence what is on the agenda. An agreed-upon document should describe how the meeting dates are set, the agenda made, and the meetings run. Some suggestions:

- Set the dates of all staff meetings before the academic year begins.
- Choose the same days of each month to help with calendar management.
- Attendance at staff meetings is expected.
- Define a quorum, and how a meeting is canceled.
- The meeting does not need to be led by the Director, but can be led by a staff member elected for the year.
- The Director's role could vary from being the meeting leader, to a member of the group, or to the note taker.
- The Director determines the process for setting the agenda, based on staff and administrative suggestions.
- Define what group business is and handle the rest outside of a staff meeting.
- Put the agenda on the intranet, or e-mail it, several days in advance.
- Each agenda item should have a document for discussion or action. Staff should be prepared by having read ahead of time. There should be no surprises on the agenda.
- Agenda, documents, and notes are then archived on the intranet.

Project the Agenda

One effective way for a group to stay on task during a staff meeting is to project the agenda and supporting documents. It is also good to have someone take notes throughout the meeting. The document under discussion will be on the screen for all to see (and on the laptops/tablets of individuals). Digressions are usually avoided. The person taking notes captures what is said as it is said. All can see what the note taker writes, and hence the time to edit the notes is when they are on the screen. Decisions are recorded as they are made. The meeting minutes are then saved to the library intranet.

Respect the Time of Others

To respect the time of others, all individual and group meetings need to start and end on time. The meeting should start on time even if not everyone is present. Talk privately with latecomers. In addition to respecting the time of others, starting and ending meetings on time is a very desirable core value. It reinforces a tone of professionalism among the staff. A casual attitude about time can carry over into other work, and that is not good for a library.

Project Management Format

Every idea for a change, no matter how small, should be written out in a simple project management format, reviewed and understood by everyone who likely will be affected by that change. Only then, and depending on decision-making norms, should a decision be made and recorded. Anything less than this will eventually lead to problems, and perhaps no internal support when poor decisions and a lack of accountability points directly to the administrator in charge.

READING

STANDARDS AND GUIDELINES

Association of College and Research Libraries. "Standards for Libraries in Higher Education." Chicago: American Library Association, 2011. www.ala.org/acrl/standards/standardslibraries.

ADVICE AND RESEARCH

Alire, Camila A., and G. Edward Evans. *Academic Librarianship*. New York: Neal-Schuman Publishers, Inc., 2010.

Garvin, David A., and Michael A. Roberto. "What You Don't Know About Making Decisions." In *Harvard Business Review on Managing Projects*. Boston: Harvard Business Press, 2005.

Giesecke, Joan, and Beth McNeil. *Fundamentals of Library Supervision*. Chicago: American Library Association, 2005.

Oncken, William, Jr., and Donald L. Wass. "Management Time: Who's Got the Monkey?" In *HBR's 10 Must Reads on Managing Yourself*. Boston: Harvard Business Review Press, 2010.

16
Communication

Internal and External Messages

ASSERTION

The academic library Director understands that the amount, timeliness, and integrity of the communications between the Director and the library staff, and the campus community, are foundational for the success of his or her tenure.

COMMENTARY

Administrative Communication Style

Effective administrators learn the norms for communicating in an institution by paying attention to effective leaders. Normally, their written and oral comments tend to be short. Around a table, they add a phrase to the discussion, not a paragraph. In a meeting, they know whose meeting it is, respect someone else's agenda, and don't talk too much. In writing, they start with the point, use bullet points, and always say less than they could. They rarely try to be funny in writing, and certainly not at the expense of a staff member. Effective administrators learn the norms for communication in their institutions, and those who don't speak or write this way find themselves either not invited, or if invited not listened to.

Update Meetings

A basic way the Director can build and sustain a working relationship (at the right level of trust) with librarians and other key staff is to have regularly scheduled, individual update meetings. Talking privately with individuals is a basic part of an administrator's job.

In small-staff libraries, where having a scheduled update meeting may seem silly, the Director should nevertheless schedule them. The structure of a defined day and time suggests that the Director and a fellow librarian shouldn't just "talk business" whenever it occurs to one of them. Rather, most topics can wait until the next meeting. It is often better to wait, to think, to prepare, and to talk in an office according to a schedule. That may not be how some people prefer to operate, but it may be better for the operation of the library.

In libraries with one administrator, the update meetings are between the Director and each librarian, and some others who may not be librarians, such as the lead person for Access Services, Technology, and the Administrative Assistant. In larger libraries with several administrators, the update meetings are between department heads and librarians, and the Director and administrators and other key people.

The purpose of an individual update meeting is about two-way communication, and not really about control. The administrator and the person have a chance to talk about current projects, how well those are going, what tasks are upcoming, what support the person may need from the administrator, and if there are any other issues. This is also the time for the administrator to outline what he or she is thinking about or working on. An individual update meeting is the best way for a Director to understand how his or her leadership is perceived, glimpse the morale of some staff, and hear things that would otherwise not be said.

Sending E-mails

Experience teaches if it is better to communicate in person or in writing with certain individuals, certain groups, or regarding certain content. The advantage to communicating through e-mail is that it can be kept by either party and subsequently referred to. Lessons everyone should learn about writing e-mails in the workplace are even more important for an administrator:

- Write e-mails that are short, to the point, and without errors.
- Reread the e-mail before sending it. How might it be misunderstood (words and tone)?
- The e-mail might be forwarded. Is there anything in the e-mail that shouldn't be there?

An administrator should consider the value of interpersonal relationships with staff. Will sending an e-mail (or some form of social media) cause more problems than not sending it?

Replying to E-mails

To manage the quantity of daily emails, administrators often weigh the value of acknowledging e-mails from known senders, compared to the time it takes to reply. Whether an individual acknowledges an e-mail develops an impression of that person. Is the recipient too busy, or too important to write a few words of acknowledgement? There are plenty of busy and important people who reply briefly to e-mails, or have an Administrative Assistant do that. A reply indicates that the message was received and acknowledged. The absence of a reply could mean several things, and none of them positive. An administrator needs to decide on an approach to replying to e-mails from people they know. If the default position is to not reply, then that will create a different image than if the default position is to reply.

Meetings

Meetings are for communication and decision-making. Low-level communication (e.g., announcements) is better done in writing. The Director needs to monitor the amount of time staff are spending in meetings, and the value of what occurs. Count the salaries in a room and ask if the business of this meeting is worth that much money. E-mail and individual update meetings are more likely to accomplish certain things with less disruption to staff time.

Marketing

An academic library is going to be used well or not depending on the quality of the collection, staff, buildings, and technology. Marketing on behalf of the library cannot mask what isn't there. However, there are ways to promote library services to faculty and students, and that takes an intentional marketing and communications plan. Work with the whole library staff on any marketing effort, and especially on learning how to talk positively about the library and its services. Have an advertising budget and ignore complaints about spending money on advertising.

APPLICATION

Types of Communication

Communication between the academic library Director and the library staff needs to occur through recurring meetings, written updates, and written e-mails when there is a need to know.

In small-staff libraries:

Recurring all-staff meetings. Meetings which are short (half-hour), often (weekly), and scheduled are better than infrequent, long, and unscheduled meetings. However, if there aren't agenda items, it is always better to cancel a meeting in advance.

Individual meetings with the Director. Short (fifteen to thirty minutes), often (weekly or biweekly), and scheduled is better than unscheduled and infrequent.

In medium- to large-staff libraries:

Individual update meetings between the Director and direct reports. Half-hour, biweekly, scheduled meetings are best for good communication.

Staff meetings with the Director. The content of an all-staff meeting needs to be worth the time and effort of bringing people together (compared to written communication).

Ad hoc e-mails from the Director to the whole staff. It is important to update everyone on things which are time-sensitive and out of the ordinary. Staff shouldn't be left to wonder and speculate ("Why are there workers outside my office, what are they fixing, and how come nobody told me?").

A monthly summary e-mail of past news, and the dates of upcoming events. This is the Director's formal way of making sure that everyone got the same information.

The goal is for the Director to be transparent with the staff about things which affect the staff (and which are their business), to tell the staff what is known and can be shared, and to tell them "now." Further, the reason to write a monthly summary (especially with calendar items) and archive it on the library intranet is so that everyone knows what has happened or is upcoming. No one should complain that "They never tell us anything."

Update Meeting Logistics

If the academic library administrator and librarians do not think the recurring update meetings are a good use of time, then before ending these meetings they ought to ask themselves if they are using this time in productive ways. There may be a need for mutual teaching about the point of these meetings, how to prepare, and the best way to work through agendas. Sometimes an update meeting is short, and that is acceptable if indeed there isn't much to talk about. It is better to have a regularly scheduled day and time, and meet for a short time, rather than to meet only when someone requests.

The administrator and the librarian should each prepare their own agendas for each meeting. The librarian should start the meeting and outline what he or she has been working on and how well it has gone, and then talk about tasks for upcoming weeks. This is also the time to talk about personal issues which impinge on work. The administrator will have other items to ask about. It is desirable to use a common template for agendas, based on the categories in an annual work plan. Agendas should be kept either on an individual's server space or on shared intranet space. For the meeting, some people prefer viewing each other's agenda on a large screen. Others prefer to keep agendas on their own paper or laptop/tablet. Each should take notes, and be clear at the end about the "to do" items. These should be revisited at subsequent update meetings. Notes from these meetings roll into preparation for annual evaluations.

Marketing Assistance

In devising a marketing plan, always include someone from the campus Communications office. That person knows about branding, production, and distribution. Establish a budget line for advertising. Advertising to students doesn't always cost, and the Communications group has existing ways to get messages to students. Additionally, there might be a faculty member who teaches marketing, and who has students looking for a project or an internship. Obtaining help from people who know how to market should result in unique and effective ideas, a disciplined plan, and some "know how" to make it happen. ACRL also has ideas for "marketing @ your library."

Branding

An academic library may have some minimal branding, and that is best seen as advertising. For example, individual librarian pages on the website will probably be templates branded as part of the library site (with the wrapper making it clear that the library is part of the institution). There will likely be library letterhead. Perhaps the library will have other items with the branding of the institution and library. For example, it is common to put a container of pencils next to public computers. Have the library URL printed on pencils, and encourage students to take them. Many libraries have plastic book bags at the Circulation Desk for rainy days. Print the library URL on these bags and view the cost as advertising. Think of what else you can give away which is branded marketing.

Calendar

It should be non-negotiable that the whole library staff use and keep up-to-date the institutional calendaring software. Individuals need to use this so that others can see when they are available. Equally important, if everyone uses the software, then the library Administrative Assistant can put on everyone's calendar the dates which all staff need to know (e.g., times the library is closed, or staff meetings).

READING

STANDARDS AND GUIDELINES

Association of College and Research Libraries. "Standards for Libraries in Higher Education." Chicago: American Library Association, 2011. www.ala.org/acrl/standards/standardslibraries.

ADVICE AND RESEARCH

Alire, Camila A., and G. Edward Evans. *Academic Librarianship.* New York: Neal-Schuman Publishers, Inc., 2010.

Giesecke, Joan, and Beth McNeil. *Fundamentals of Library Supervision.* Chicago: American Library Association, 2005.

Bartheld, Eric. "Listen Up, Librarians. It's All About the Message." In *The Expert Library: Staffing, Sustaining, and Advancing the Academic Library in the 21st Century,* edited by Scott Walter and Karen Williams. Chicago: American Library Association, 2010.

"Marketing @ your library." Chicago: Association of College and Research Libraries. www.ala.org/acrl/issues/marketing.

McCarthy, Dan. "How to Have an Effective 1 on 1." Great Leadership blog, March 2, 2009. www.greatleadershipbydan.com/2009/03/how-to-have-effective-1 -on-1.html.

Ross, Catherine Sheldrick, and Kirsti Nilsen. *Communicating Professionally: A How-To-Do-It Manual for Librarians,* 3rd ed. Chicago: ALA Neal-Schuman, 2013.

Stanley, John. "Improving Communications Skills." In *It's All About Student Learning. Managing Community and Other College Libraries in the 21st Century,* edited by David R. Dowell and Gerard B. McCabe. Westport, CT: Libraries Unlimited, 2006.

Woodward, Jeannette. *Creating the Customer-Driven Academic Library.* Chicago: American Library Association, 2009.

17
The Tone

Desirable and Productive Workplace

ASSERTION

The academic library Director understands that individual and staff performance will improve over time if he or she is an encourager, and intentionally promotes a positive tone in order to make the library a desirable and productive workplace.

COMMENTARY

Encourage

When calibrating the job performance of individuals against expectations, the academic library Director should err on the side of encouragement, both in private and in more public ways. It is important to compliment individuals on their work, to publicly say "thank you" when projects are finished, and to daily encourage staff. That requires being intentional. Being an encourager does not mean ignoring the shortcomings of individuals or of a group. The Director needs to talk in private about areas for improvement. It is quite possible to work with individuals on improving some aspect of work, while at the same time sustaining a culture of encouraging staff to do well (and noticing when it occurs).

Morale

The Director sets the tone for working in the library. The Director should learn what to notice in order to understand the morale level of library personnel. The degree to which some individuals care about their work can change, and part of an administrative job is noticing a change in attitude and trying to understand the causes. Are there under-the-surface resentments? Do some staff think they are on the team, and others not? Is there a situation external to work, but which spills over into work? An academic library administrator needs to learn when to isolate issues, when to respond, and when not to over-react. Walk around the library, talk to staff, stay positive, be generous with compliments, and do little things that make the library a desirable place to work.

Details

Paying attention to workplace details makes a difference in staff attitude. If an administrator expects a high quality of work from staff, then they need top-quality work conditions. It is much better to eliminate things that irritate staff, rather than downplaying the complaint ("That's how it is. Deal with it"). There are things an administrator can and should do to solve workplace issues, from physical conditions to workload to interpersonal irritations. By solving an issue for one person there is a message for the whole staff: "When you work here, we don't put up with second-rate conditions. There are no excuses for poor working conditions, and we can fix this." The corollary for providing good working conditions is an expectation of high job performance. The two are closely inter-connected.

Social

An academic library doesn't have to be a "fun" place to work, but it also doesn't have to be so serious that people can't enjoy the company of other staff. There should be times built into the calendar when staff are together socially. There could be regularly scheduled social gatherings and celebrations of important moments in the lives of staff, including when student workers achieve something notable.

Staff Room

Every library needs a staff room which is both for eating and also for small group socializing. The quality of the staff room matters to some people's attitude about working in the library. How the room looks, and what is available make a difference. A desirable staff room is necessary for small social gatherings, and that helps make the library a good place to work.

Staff Perceptions

Morale is related to most staff agreeing that the administrators are doing the necessary background work so that staff can do their jobs at a certain level of quality. When that happens, then morale should be neutral to positive. If the perception is shared that the Director is politically ineffective, not trying very hard to be a campus-wide advocate for the library, or plays favorites among library staff, then a malaise will set in among some. Once that happens, the Director will have a problem with managing the whole staff.

Resolving Problems

An administrator's job is either to resolve problems, or see that those directly involved resolve their own problems. An administrator should not preside over a culture where problems of all varieties linger, are ignored, or are considered intractable. Corrosive to a staff are individuals whose experiences cause them to believe "It is what it is" and "We tried that, it didn't work, and there is no point in trying again." An administrator wants to create an expectation that problems can and will be resolved, or at least a good effort will be made.

It is not desirable to work in a culture where staff expect that an administrator needs to be directly involved in the resolution of all issues. The dilemmas that seem intractable, have a long history, and are clearly affecting job performance will need administrative intervention. Lots of other issues need to be resolved by those people who "own" that issue. An administrator's job is to create an expectation that problems will be resolved, that those people involved will solve most of their issues, and that there is a high threshold for when an administrator needs to get involved.

An Attitude of "Yes"

The Director can influence morale by creating a culture among the staff where "yes" is the default starting point when thinking through an answer. Talking about what is possible is better than reviewing what someone thinks can't be done. The Director needs to identify and reduce (or eliminate) the sour attitudes and the "historians" who use past practices to limit present options. The Director needs to model an attitude of "Let's look into that and see what our options are."

Slow to Say "No"

Administrators should challenge staff in the habit of quickly giving negative responses to overtures for library services. Patrons should not hear excuses, apologies, or blame. Quick negative responses create a perception that neither administrators nor individuals on the library staff can set priorities, reallocate resources, or manage staff time very well. It is better for staff to learn to reply to a patron with some variant of "Let me find the answer, or some way to resolve this."

Passive and Abstract Words

Administrators should be aware of whether or not they blame abstractions for why things are the way they are (e.g., "Budget said . . ."). Listen also for instances of cause and effect referred to in the passive tense (e.g., "Somebody did this to us"). If administrators blame abstractions instead of citing real people by name, and talk about things happening to the library in the passive tense, then the library staff who are used to talking, thinking, and acting that way will be reinforced, and continue to do so. Conversely, if administrators set the example of citing the names of real people instead of abstractions, and describe who made a decision (and how it was made) instead of blaming things as if they are out of anyone's control, then that is modeling the way for library staff to talk, think, and act. It is better when library staff talk to patrons as if things are within the control of real people who can make decisions. The words used influence how the library staff talks, thinks, and acts.

Slow to Take Credit

The Director should be slow to take credit, even when deserved, and instead look for ways to share credit with library staff for large and small accomplishments. It is best to find oral and written ways to give credit to others. It is also good to let others write the announcement or give the talk. A Director should be conscious of how much public airtime he or she is taking, and how instead others on the library staff might have some recognition. Understanding and practicing the importance of humility are powerful components of an effective leader.

APPLICATION

Work Space Conditions

If a desk chair is a wrong fit for someone, then the academic library administrator needs to replace the chair to improve ergonomics, or obtain adjustable-height desks. Or if the temperature in work spaces is too cold or too hot, then buy some digital thermometers, take readings, and share that data with someone in the Facilities department to improve the HVAC system. Buy some space heaters, too. Know when there are things about the work space that bother some individuals, and then do something about solving the problem. Citing a lack of money, or "others will want a new one too" are hollow answers to an employee whose back hurts or whose office is too cold. Part of an administrator's job is to create an expectation that work space conditions will be such that people can do their jobs well. If there are irritants, then effective administrators get personally involved, obtain some data, work the system politically, and stay with that issue until it is fixed.

Solving Inherited Issues

Some issues that come to the academic library Director's attention are inherited. Solving a lingering problem may require the help of a decision-maker external to the library who shares an attitude of "Neither one of us made this problem, but let's see if together we can resolve it." A good way to approach a long-standing problem is to write its history, complete with documents, and see if all parties agree on this description. If staff can understand how an issue came to be, then maybe the relevant players can see a way to craft a solution. Write out a proposed solution, and work with the staff for comment.

Social

There are staff social occasions that don't cost much money. It is easier to have simple occasions and hold them in the library during the workday, rather than expecting people to go somewhere after hours (and pay the bill). Some libraries have spaces that would work for a staff party after the term has ended and there aren't patrons around.

Staff Room

A well-appointed staff room needs a:

- dishwasher,
- set of dishes and flatware,

- microwave, and
- refrigerator.

Providing dishes, flatware, and a dishwasher solves a lot of petty issues. It is also healthier than a sink of dirty dishes. Having a dishwasher is worth it, whatever it costs, and however it is paid for.

READING

STANDARDS AND GUIDELINES

Association of College and Research Libraries. "Standards for Libraries in Higher Education." Chicago: American Library Association, 2011. www.ala.org/acrl/standards/standardslibraries.

ADVICE AND RESEARCH

Bakker, Arnold B., ed. *Advances in Positive Organizational Psychology, Volume 1.* Bingley, England: Emerald Group Publishing Limited, 2013.

Amabile, Teresa. "How to Kill Creativity." In *Harvard Business Review on Managing Projects.* Boston: Harvard Business Press, 2005.

Ancona, Deborah, Thomas W. Malone, Wanda J. Orlikowski, and Peter M. Senge. "In Praise of the Incomplete Leader." In *HBR's 10 Must Reads on Leadership.* Boston: Harvard Business Review Press, 2011.

Collins, Jim. "Level 5 Leadership: The Triumph of Humility and Fierce Resolve." In *HBR's 10 Must Reads on Leadership.* Boston: Harvard Business Review Press, 2011.

Giesecke, Joan, and Beth McNeil. *Fundamentals of Library Supervision.* Chicago: American Library Association, 2005.

Goffee, Robert, and Gareth Jones. "Why Should Anyone Be Led by You?" In *HBR's 10 Must Reads on Leadership.* Boston: Harvard Business Review Press, 2011.

Goleman, Daniel, Richard Boyatzis, and Annie McKee. "Primal Leadership: The Hidden Driver of Great Performance." In *HBR's 10 Must Reads on Managing Yourself.* Boston: Harvard Business Review Press, 2010.

Goleman, Daniel. "What Makes a Leader?" In *HBR's 10 Must Reads on Leadership.* Boston: Harvard Business Review Press, 2011.

Oncken, William Jr., and Donald L. Wass. "Management Time: Who's Got the Monkey?" In *HBR's 10 Must Reads on Managing Yourself.* Boston: Harvard Business Review Press, 2010.

18
How Are You?

Issues of Health and Well-Being

ASSERTION

The academic library Director is aware of the health and well-being of all who work in the library, and when appropriate, asks "How are you?" including of himself or herself.

COMMENTARY

Staff

Periodically asking after the health and well-being of library staff is important because the academic library Director ought to care about all of the people who work in the library, and may learn of reasons for concern. All academic library administrators need to be attuned to clues about when changes in an individual's physical or mental health are affecting work. Or the job performance may be fine, but things aren't going well outside of work. There are guidelines from the Human Resources department about confidentiality, and the Director needs to know that an honest answer may not be forthcoming. If the administrator has built a relationship of trust, especially through update meetings, then a staff member may well choose to give an honest (and confidential) answer if things are not going well. If not, then the administrator needs to stay closely attuned and continue to provide opportunities for conversation.

Director's Health

The Director needs to monitor his or her physical health, family situation, mental and emotional well-being, and overall attitude toward the job. A library Director position can easily consume the person who holds it. It is common to work too many hours, and when not in the office, think (and worry) constantly about the staff, the safety of staff and students in the library, the budget, and campus politics. The responsibility never ends, and the job can quietly take its toll. Trying to "tough it out" will eventually hurt one's health, close relationships, the operation and status of the library, and perhaps one or more library staff members.

Sick Leave

Library staff are allocated sick leave because it is good for their health to stay home when sick, and it is good for the health of their co-workers (and the library patrons) that they not be in the building. As Director, remind staff to stay home when ill, and especially when contagious. An administrator may need to counsel an ill employee to go home. It is too easy for dedicated library staff to think they are indispensable and must be on the job, even when ill. When administrators are ill, then they need to admit the obvious and model good behavior by going home.

Annual Leave

An institutional policy manual should explain why annual leave is granted, and define the circumstances under which vacation may be taken. Vacation is commonly understood to be granted because it is good for the employee, but with the dates approved by an administrator. Normally vacation should not be taken during a school term. If there is a compelling reason why vacation days are requested during a term, then the Director should have a good reason for approval. To go on vacation while school is in session sends the wrong message to co-workers, students, faculty, and other campus administrators about the necessity of having a fully staffed library during academic terms. Administrators should also avoid taking vacation while school is in session.

APPLICATION

Take Care of Yourself

Managing an academic library can consume the person doing it. There really isn't a way to do it "part time." It is important to do things for the good of an academic library administrator's physical and emotional health. Watch what others in similar positions do, and copy what seems beneficial. For example, get up out of the desk chair at regular intervals. Find excuses to take short walks in the building. Look at something other than a computer screen. Go to the gym during lunch. Go home at 5 p.m., at least some days. Walk outside of the library each day. Stay home when ill. Actually take vacation days. The institution gives vacation days for a good reason, with the expectation that everyone, including administrators, will use at least some of them. The list goes on. The academic library Director needs to be very intentional about taking care of oneself.

Germs

Libraries have lots of spaces that attract germs. Often someone within the institution will send a list of ways to avoid contagion. There are a few things to try in a library during times when cold and flu germs are especially prevalent:

- Affix hand sanitizer dispensers to walls.
- Place bottles of hand sanitizers throughout the library.
- Wipe keyboards daily.
- Monitor cleanliness in bathrooms and advocate for more cleaning if there is a problem.
- Post signs in bathrooms about the importance of washing hands to reduce the spread of germs.

READING

STANDARDS AND GUIDELINES

Association of College and Research Libraries. "Standards for Libraries in Higher Education." Chicago: American Library Association, 2011. www.ala.org/acrl/standards/standardslibraries.

ADVICE AND RESEARCH

Brewer, Julie. "Assisting Employees." In *Human Resource Management in Today's Academic Library,* edited by Janice Simmons-Welburn and Beth McNeil. Westport, CT: Libraries Unlimited, 2004.

Hawks, Melanie. *Life-Work Balance.* Chicago: Association of College and Research Libraries, 2008.

HBR's 10 Must Reads on Managing Yourself. Boston: Harvard Business Review Press, 2010.

Watkins, Michael. *The First 90 Days: Critical Success Strategies for New Leaders at All Levels.* Boston: Harvard Business Review Press, 2003.

19
Change

Recognizing Need and Leading Change

ASSERTION

An academic library administrator uses a project management approach to successfully lead change, developing a plan with affected staff, identifying the need for this change, and describing how this change is sustainable.

COMMENTARY

The Need for Change

The nature of both higher education and its libraries is that constant change is normal. There will be library staff who see the need to make changes in areas as disparate as building space, collections, hours, or work flow. There will be other library staff who won't like any proposed changes, and are experienced at resisting. There will also be campus leaders who look to the library budget, space, or personnel in order to solve a problem unrelated to the library. The library is nested within the institution's culture of change. The specific example may originate from within the library staff, or come from outside the library. It may have internal resistance from library staff or external resistance from campus administrators. The task of academic library administrators is to identify plausible reasons for the upcoming change, convey a realistic sense of urgency, make a plan with those affected, and move.

When the administrator attempts to lead a group, or the whole staff, through some proposed change, then it is wise to identify:

- what needs to change in the library,
- why that change is necessary,
- a solution (or two),
- the fiscal and staff price,
- how that process will occur, and
- how that change can be sustained.

Basic to success is identifying the reason for a change. Is this coming from an administrator because that is how that person wants something done? Or are there external forces that are bringing about the need for change, such as budget, governance, technology, publishing, teaching and learning, or accreditation? Without some data, and plausible cause and effect, then it is harder for some staff to see why they should invest in this effort. The change also needs to be viewed as something which will likely last. Why should anyone spend time, effort, and emotional energy on changing something that appears to be "just fine" right now? Can this change really be sustained in terms of the budget, staff time, or political capital?

Project Management

Administrators need to view every proposed change in the library space, operations, and services in "project management" terms. Whether a small, simple alteration or a complicated change, what is proposed needs to be written in a project management format. For simple changes, perhaps only a few items need to be addressed (e.g., what is proposed, who is involved, budget, and timeline). Nevertheless, it is wise that each change in the library be outlined. An administrator needs to make sure that the information is correct, and then circulate it to affected staff where it will be vetted. Think through a change, plan it with staff, and be sure that all affected people know of a change before taking action. By viewing changes in "project management" terms, mistakes should be minimized, the process for making decisions strengthened, and the likelihood of success increased.

Price of Change

While doing preliminary thinking about a change, and before "going public" with the library staff, discuss this with the Provost and make sure the library can afford the price of this change. Is there political and budgetary support, and is the rationale sufficient to sustain this change over time? Do not start a change process without a high level of confidence that it will succeed, and that the political price will not be too high. If the academic library Director starts several efforts which fail (or succeed but at a cost which is too high), then that person's effectiveness may be compromised. Some staff will view the next plan warily. The Provost may privately question the leadership of the library. On the other hand, with some success leading change projects, then staff who grudgingly tolerated that project may need to reevaluate the wisdom of their opposition. Success makes it harder for recalcitrant staff to stay that way.

Timeframe

Any project needs plenty of time built into it to involve and prepare affected staff for whatever is coming. Changes which are perceived by some staff to be abrupt, or imposed without staff involvement, will be difficult for those staff to accept, even if the change was the right thing to do. Be generous with the variable of time.

Consultant

An external library consultant can be of considerable help in many library change processes. The consultant can and will say things which are politically hard for the Director to say, simply because the consultant has no connections to the people on the library staff and will go away. That is useful, if the consultant's message is valid, the staff are prepared, and the solutions seem viable. The use of a consultant often indicates to staff that administrators have been thinking about a change well before staff are included, and that other libraries are also dealing with this proposed change.

APPLICATION

Project Management Template

Create a project management template, and expect that staff will use some parts of it when proposing any change in the library space, operations, or services. The template needs to include:

- what is proposed,
- who has the lead,
- who else is involved,
- who will be affected,

- timeline,
- budget,
- decision-making process,
- training,
- ongoing responsibility for implementation, and
- evaluation and closure.

Keep this template on the library intranet.

Updates

Frequent updates on the progress of any project are really helpful to those involved. Show the benchmarks and the timeline. This helps with those whose attitudes range from indifferent to skeptical. Regular updates show that this project is actually under way, and is going to happen.

READING

STANDARDS AND GUIDELINES

Association of College and Research Libraries. "Standards for Libraries in Higher Education." Chicago: American Library Association, 2011. www.ala.org/acrl/standards/standardslibraries.

ADVICE AND RESEARCH

Alire, Camila A. and G. Edward Evans. *Academic Librarianship.* New York: Neal-Schuman Publishers, Inc., 2010.

Applegate, Rachel. *Managing the Small College Library.* Santa Barbara, CA: Libraries Unlimited, 2010.

The Essentials of Project Management: Business Literacy for HR Professionals. Boston: Harvard Business Press, 2006.

Giesecke, Joan, and Beth McNeil. *Fundamentals of Library Supervision.* Chicago: American Library Association, 2005.

HBR's 10 Must Reads on Change Management. Boston: Harvard Business Review Press, 2011.

Managing Change and Transition. Boston: Harvard Business Review Press, 2003.

Managing Projects Large and Small. The Fundamental Skills for Delivering on Budget and on Time. Boston: Harvard Business School Press, 2004.

Watkins, Michael. *The First 90 Days: Critical Success Strategies for New Leaders at All Levels.* Boston: Harvard Business Review Press, 2003.

20

Errors in Judgment

Understanding and Learning

ASSERTION

The academic library Director admits errors in judgment, changes course if something isn't working, tries to understand the correct reasons, and shares with staff what was learned from that experience.

COMMENTARY

Reducing Likely Mistakes

Minimizing likely mistakes is part of any administrator's work. The academic library Director especially needs to say "no" when someone proposes a project or idea that seems unlikely to succeed. The Director may understand something about the campus political context, the budget, contract language, or interpersonal relationships that will stymie this project. The need to say "no" is to avoid wasting the time and effort of staff, spending money with minimal return, and diminishing some of the credibility of those involved.

Errors in judgment have a cumulative effect. Failed projects lead to a negative perception of the Director's judgment, discourage staff, and build an undesirable image of the library. Being associated with more than a few mistakes casts doubt on an academic library administrator's judgment. It is better not to let staff start on a project which has a low chance of success. Judgment about when not to start something comes from experience with similar projects and perhaps from conversations with other experienced administrators.

The Underside

Mistakes for which the Director takes the blame are usually either errors in judgment, or events out of the Director's control. Additionally, not everyone on the library staff or in the institution wants the Director or the library to be successful. There may well be people with influence who don't like the Director personally, or who don't see the need for the library program to have all that it currently does. Competitors would rather have some library space and budget reallocated.

Without being obsessed with "enemies," it is nevertheless important for the Director to understand correctly who is in competition with the library program, what they want, and why. If the opposition is personal to the Director, then the Provost needs to intervene or else there will be longer-term damage to the library program. If the opposition is to the value and performance of the library relative to the investment, then that requires a different approach. It is important to understand who wants some of the library's budget, space, or scope of activity, what they want, and why.

APPLICATION

Admitting Errors

It is desirable that the academic library Director admits an error in judgment, and either ends or alters something which isn't going well. How that is done matters. The update meetings are times when the academic library administrator can ask individuals if an initiative is going sideways, and if so, what to do about it. Individual conversations are useful for determining next steps, and for support of key staff. When ending an initiative, send out a terse e-mail, explain why you are ending something, take the blame (at least, don't blame others), and outline a timeline to end a project. Data to help correctly understand cause and effect is helpful. Any explanation for changing course on a project needs to be clearly heard (or written), and understood by the staff.

READING

ADVICE AND RESEARCH

Fritts, Jack E., Jr., *Mistakes in Academic Library Management: Grievous Errors and How to Avoid Them*. Lanham, MD: Scarecrow Press, 2009.

Heifetz, Ronald A., and Marty Linsky. "A Survival Guide for Leaders." In *HBR's 10 Must Reads on Change Management*. Boston: Harvard Business Review Press, 2011.

Kotter, John P. "Leading Change. Why Transformation Efforts Fail." In *HBR's 10 Must Reads on Change Management*. Boston: Harvard Business Review Press, 2011.

Managing Change and Transition. Boston: Harvard Business Review Press, 2003.

Manzoni, Jean-Francois, and Jean-Louis Barsoux. "The Set-Up-to-Fail Syndrome." In *HBR's 10 Must Reads on Managing People*. Boston: Harvard Business Review Press, 2011.

Staw, Barry M., and Jerry Ross. "Knowing When to Pull the Plug." In *Harvard Business Review on Managing Projects*. Boston: Harvard Business Press, 2005.

21
Ending

Making a Transition

ASSERTION

The academic library Director knows that how he or she ends time in a position is not only personally important, but also important for the transition that will be made by the library staff and the incoming new Director.

COMMENTARY

Time to Leave

The academic library Director needs to know when it is time to leave a position, both for his or her own good, but also for the good of the institution. Ideally, the Director should leave when things are going well professionally within the library, and going well personally (e.g., with one's health and personal life). That isn't always possible. It is, however, usually possible for the Director to make the decision to leave, rather than realizing (too late) that last year was the time to leave.

Advance Notice

If leaving for a new job, then the timing of that hiring process is set by the receiving institution. It is wise to tell the Provost early if engaged in serious conversations with another institution. That may not be good news to the Provost, but informing the Provost late in a process is usually worse. The Provost will likely need to find an interim solution on short notice.

If retirement is the reason for leaving, then the Provost should know during the preceding academic year, and publicly announce in the autumn of the Director's last academic year. That usually provides enough time for a search, which, if it goes well, should ideally result in a new hire and a summer transition. If the search occurs too late in the "hiring season," then there is the higher likelihood of missing a summer transition. While having an interim Director for a year isn't bad, it does nevertheless create a period of reduced political influence for the library.

For the Director Personally

A leadership transition is important for the institution, the library, and for the Director's personal sense of validation of the work done. The decision to leave for another job, or to retire, is personally an important one for the Director. Whether or not the Director's tenure has been good for the institution, the library staff, and the Director personally, it is nevertheless important to acknowledge that service. A pat on the back can shape a Director's attitude toward the institution for years to come, and that can have beneficial consequences.

For the Staff

The conditions under which the Director leaves set the tone and agenda for the new Director. Staff will watch the circumstances under which the Director leaves. That will serve as a proxy indicator of the value top administrators place on the library. If the manner in which a Director leaves is supportive, then that will add to the perception among many staff about the value of their work. The converse is also true. At best, the last months of a Director's tenure should prepare the staff for an orderly transition.

For the New Director

The context for the new Director is set in part by how the previous Director leaves. The current Director needs to set the agenda for the last months with the goal of a good transition. Either the new Director walks into a neutral or positive situation, or the new Director starts with a set of problems. The new Director didn't create the issues he or she inherits, but will have to respond to them at some point. The best situation is when the current Director is able to minimize the "fix it" agenda for the new Director.

Succession Planning

If a librarian shows leadership potential, or an Associate Director is ready to lead a library, then it is wise to invest in that person and help with administrative and leadership skills. It doesn't mean that the person will necessarily move into an open position. The established hiring process needs to be followed. The mentoring and guiding efforts may result in producing a good administrator for another library. How a person is chosen for a position matters, and so an in-house candidate needs to be especially vetted.

APPLICATION

Knowing When

How do you know when it is time to leave an academic library Director's position, whether retiring or looking for a new job? The answers to three basic questions should help:

- Ask yourself if you have come "close enough" to doing what you were hired to accomplish.
- Ask yourself if staying one more year would make any difference in finishing that "to do" list, or not. If most of the items are now checked off, and if the remaining items are not likely to be completed in one more year, then more time isn't the decisive variable. It is a good time to leave, both for your sake and for the sake of the library.
- Ask yourself if a likely successor is "out there." If so, and there is a high probability of a good transition to a new Director, then that is another compelling reason to leave. Indeed, the new Director may not need to finish your checklist, but will have a new one.

While people also factor in health, financial considerations, and, if retiring, ask "What will I do with myself?" the three questions above seem basic and sufficient for deciding when to leave. These three considerations are more likely about a good transition for the library.

Making the Announcement

How should the Director tell the library staff that he or she is leaving? It is better to make the announcement in person at a staff meeting rather than by e-mail. Further, the announcement should be made together with the Provost.

At a regular or special staff meeting, the Director should make a short statement about leaving, the Provost follow with words of thanks, and then conclude with a comment about the upcoming search process. Having the Provost in attendance sends a message to the library staff: "This upcoming leadership transition is important to the whole institution (not just to the library staff). That is why I am here helping to make this announcement. Further, I am in charge of the process by which the new Director will be chosen." This personal announcement can then be followed up with an e-mail to the campus community from the Provost.

Finish Strong

The time between the announcement and departure may result in the Director being perceived as a "lame duck." One effect of uncertainty about future leadership is that one or several of the best people in the library might leave for other jobs. It is rational behavior to accept a position elsewhere rather than stay and be part of a transition to an unknown new leader. Other effects might be putting projects on hold, or some of the staff taking it easy.

The best way to keep everyone working at the right level is for the Director to remain engaged and on-the-job until the announced last day. When the Director is asked if he or she is counting the days, the response should be "No," followed by clarity that there are no "lame ducks" working in this library. Working diligently to the end, not letting daily routines slide, and in all respects remaining as the Director are all important for the transition. People remember what was done between the public announcement that one is leaving, and the date when one actually leaves. "Finish strong" is a cliché that actually matters.

Celebrate

When a library Director leaves, that person's work ought to be celebrated throughout the institution, and not just by the library staff. It is the Provost's role to organize an event, invite faculty, staff, administrators, and library administrators from neighboring institutions. The library's constituency is wide-reaching, and the institution ought to celebrate a Director's tenure. The message conveyed through an event hosted by the Provost is that what has been familiar and known is coming to an end, somebody else will be the Director, and that leadership of the library is the business of the Provost (on behalf of the whole institution).

READING

ADVICE AND RESEARCH

Evans, G. Edward, and Patricia Layzell Ward. *Beyond the Basics. The Management Guide for Library and Information Professionals.* New York: Neal-Schuman Publishers, Inc., 2003.

Singer, Paula M., and Gail Griffith. *Succession Planning in the Library: Developing Leaders, Managing Change.* Chicago: American Library Association, 2010.

Stueart, Robert D., and Maureen Sullivan. *Developing Library Leaders: A How-To-Do-It Manual for Coaching, Team Building, and Mentoring Library Staff.* New York: Neal-Schuman Publishers, Inc., 2010.

PART III
Supervising Operations

Part III is about the academic library Director's role in supervising the daily operations of the library. The Director needs to know just enough about disparate topics to be confident that people working in those areas are making acceptable decisions, implementing procedures, and know what to do when something fails. Doing that well is dependent on first being politically effective (Part I) and managing and leading staff well (Part II). If things are not done acceptably in those areas, then the daily operation of the library is compromised.

22
Budget

Spending It All

ASSERTION

The academic library Director is responsible for knowing the institution's accounting practices and timelines so that the library budget is made, monitored, and spent in full by the close of each fiscal year.

COMMENTARY

Budget Essentials

Basic to the academic library Director's ability to successfully manage all aspects of the library's operation is preparing, monitoring, and completely spending the library budget each fiscal year. Preparing, monitoring, and spending are linked. If spending goes over budget, then the Director has a number of problems to resolve. Some are within the library (e.g., which end-of-year invoices to not pay in order to close under budget), and some are with his or her supervisor. It is important to know the consequences to the library budget (and to the Director's political reputation) of closing the fiscal year in the red. Does a deficit carry over to the next fiscal year? What does an over-spent library budget do to the Provost's budget?

The ability to close the fiscal year closely under budget begins with know-ing the timelines for budget preparation, being successful when requesting more money, monitoring and projecting spending accurately, and then know-ing techniques for closing the fiscal year barely in the black. If the library does not spend all of its allocation, then asking for more money during the bud-get-making period has little credibility. The Director needs to establish proce-dures and provide oversight in order to spend, monitor, project, and close the fiscal year. Failing to manage the budget correctly has consequences for the Director personally and for library budgets in subsequent years.

Budget Accountability

The Director is accountable to the Provost for the management of the library budget. The Provost cares that the library budget finishes in the black, but is normally not much interested in the details. How much money is in each line, how much has been spent to date, the legitimacy and wisdom of expenditures, and any movement of money from line to line are normally the Director's business, not the Provost's.

The process for making decisions about money, and what part of the bud-get ought to be known by whom, should be clear to all staff. While all of the budget is the responsibility of the Director, not all parts are the business of the staff. For example, during the period when the fiscal year closes, making decisions about which invoices to pay in which fiscal year, and moving money from one line to another, is the business of the Director.

Purchasing and Licensing

Academic libraries spend a significant percentage of several budgetary cate-gories on licensing fees rather than as purchases. A library's budget may not reflect the change in the budget model from earlier years when content was purchased. For example, the fee to license electronic journal titles must be paid annually in order to gain access to current and back content. The Direc-tor needs to make sure that top management understands that the model changed, that licensing content must occur annually in order to keep backfiles, and that licensing has a higher and ongoing price. The budget may not have increased during the years when this transition occurred.

Spreadsheet Language

Spreadsheets, charts, and graphs are the "language" used by top administrators for communicating about budget, program evaluation, and decision-making. Academic library administrators need to communicate with top administrators using their language. That means using spreadsheets, charts, and graphs, and relatively fewer words. If administrators always summarize information using spreadsheets and colored charts, then the academic library Director should do that, too. Paragraphs of words are not the equivalent. The Director needs to be personally "good enough" at making and interpreting spreadsheets, charts, and graphs, or else the library is at a disadvantage in communicating with other campus administrators.

Proximity to Revenue

In an academic institution it is always better to be closer on the organizational chart to where revenue originates and indeed to be a unit which generates at least some revenue. That is why it is politically important that library administrators statistically show other administrators and faculty (through the governance structure) what the library budget is spent on, and that those expenditures are indeed used and valued. It is also politically helpful if library administrators personally are financial contributors to the institution. The Director should work with the Advancement office to help raise funds for the library.

APPLICATION

Budget Basics

The most important parts of the budget process to understand are:

- The timeline, decision-makers, and assumptions in the preparation of the institution's budget for the next fiscal year.
- The distinction between operating and capital budgets.
- How (and by whom) budgets are increased or decreased.
- How (and by whom) budgets are increased for inflation.
- Any idiosyncratic accounting procedures used in the institution.
- Anticipating and preparing for large capital expenses. How may unspent budget be carried over and used in subsequent fiscal years?

- Assumptions, variables, and accuracy of spreadsheets used by library staff to monitor specific parts of the budget (e.g., serials expenditures).
- The steps in the fiscal year closing period, and what can be done during these weeks in order to close the previous fiscal year in the black.
- The consequences of the library budget finishing in the red.

Budget Advice

Academic library administrators should check if these observations are legal and feasible in their institution:

The budget for the following fiscal year is generally made in the fall and early winter of the current fiscal year. Know the timeline for when to make requests, of whom, and when it is too late.

Spend all of the fiscal year's allocation. It is hard to make the case to the Provost and Budget Office personnel that the library needs more money if in fact not all of the budget is encumbered.

It is very hard to manage the budget down to zero. The best that can be done is to get close to zero or go in the red. If there are reserve or endowment funds, then cover that deficit by using those funds during the weeks after the end of the fiscal year, when there is still time to alter the closing of the fiscal year. Know how much discretionary budget can be controlled (e.g., remaining funds not yet encumbered in the current fiscal year, a reserve account, or an endowment). Then manage the budget just barely into the black at the final close, knowing that discretionary funds are there.

Inflation reduces the budget annually unless there is a way to compensate for price increases. One way to keep up with inflation is to identify contracts for services that are basic to the operation of the library. The annual increase is beyond the control of the library. Some institutions then annually increase the allocations for these contracts to keep up with inflation.

Join one or several consortia in order to lower the cost of items purchased.

The library website should always have a link to a page through which people can donate money. When someone is interested in giving money to the library, the mechanism for doing that should be evident and the process simple.

As academic library Director, set the example and be a donor of money to the library. Neither the Director nor Advancement office staff should ask other library administrators or staff to donate money. However, the Director should donate without being asked simply because that is one way to lead. As a donor, your subsequent requests to the Provost to increase the library's budget might resonate better.

If it is possible, consider selling art, artifacts, and books that aren't aligned with the library's collection policy, and put that money into endowed funds.

Annually request of the Provost increases to pay for one or several new items. If one or two are funded each fiscal year, then there is a cumulative positive effect on the budget.

Generally the Director has little discretion over pay increases, which are usually given system-wide. The Director can attempt to reclassify a position, which may result in a pay raise. Work with the Finance office to be clear about the comparison of employees to comparable positions.

Some institutions allow for putting some money in a restricted fund to then pay for large capital expenses.

Periodically request that someone from the Finance office examine all library accounting procedures, and, if there are changes to make, then implement that advice.

Is there institutional support for obtaining grants? If not, a grant may not be worth it. What will it cost in staff time to write, administer, and evaluate a grant? Before asking someone to write a grant, be clear about the cost to the library of being awarded a grant and whether or not the library can afford to accept it.

The library Director should help raise revenue for the library by soliciting gifts. Some donors prefer to give funds to be used for immediate purchases, and hence it is desirable to have a list of items and their prices. Other donors think longer-term and are supportive of endowed funds, or the naming of spaces in the library. The Advancement office should prepare a list of library spaces and the dollar amount needed to name that space.

From the institution's perspective, on-campus employment is one strategy for keeping as many students enrolled as possible. The library supports this institutional goal of a high retention rate by hiring as many student workers as possible, and paying them as much as possible. Spend all of the budget line for student workers, and, if more money is needed, then advocate for an increase in that allocation.

Service to Whom

Depending on the type of academic library, there is a need to determine the level of library service to those outside the institution. That has budget implications. There should be policy words on the library website about who does and does not have access to the building, staff time, networks, equipment, and collections.

There are several ways to think about who has access to an academic library, regardless of whether it is private or public, large or small.

Use of buildings and networks. Who has access to the library building and campus networks? The question is nested in the institution's stance toward people not connected to the institution having access to campus facilities. Academic libraries are paid for and supported in order to provide services to a defined set of people. Those outside the defined set do not necessarily have rights to use the library, unless that is part of institutional policy. Some libraries check for a campus identification card at the entrance, and only allow people with a valid ID card or a guest pass to enter. The "guest pass" is defined by staff from the library, the department that hosts guests on campus, and Information Technology (which defines and implements who has access to the wired or wireless networks).

Use of library staff time. If there is open access to a library, then the Director and librarians need to define the role of library staff (especially librarians) in working with people who are not part of that campus community. In an open-access library anyone might enter the building and expect assistance from a library staff member. Library staff time has a price tag. Some libraries instruct staff to spend only a courteous minute or two with people who are not eligible for library services.

Access to collections. Access to electronic content is often restricted by licensing agreements, limiting access to patrons in the library and those in the institution's database of students, faculty, and staff. Beyond that, access for anyone else is dependent on a budget and contractual agreement between the vendor, the Information Technology department, and the library. Sometimes alumni have access to some electronic content, but that is licensed and paid for separately. Books are usually available to alumni, or to borrowers outside the institution who purchase borrowing privileges.

Charges for Library Use

There are always precedents and implications when an academic library considers charging individuals who are not part of the campus community for use of the library. The library services for which individuals often pay (a quarterly or annual fee) are

- borrowing physical materials,
- access to the time of librarians,

- access to the library building,
- use of the network and computers within the library building, and
- access to licensed electronic content.

Sometimes schools with external programs want access for their students and faculty to another school's library building, staff, and resources. It is reasonable to expect a fee for this access. The Director and Provost need to decide if the income is worth the effort, and if there are implications for other external groups who use campus facilities. Someone in the Budget and Finance office (and perhaps legal department) should write the contract and set the level of compensation. The two schools might also create a "memorandum of understanding" for library services, even if no fee is charged.

READING

STANDARDS AND GUIDELINES

Association of College and Research Libraries. "Standards for Libraries in Higher Education." Chicago: American Library Association, 2011. www.ala.org/acrl/standards/standardslibraries.

ADVICE AND RESEARCH

Alire, Camila A., and G. Edward Evans. *Academic Librarianship.* New York: Neal-Schuman Publishers, Inc., 2010.

Applegate, Rachel. *Managing the Small College Library.* Santa Barbara, CA: Libraries Unlimited, 2010.

Barr, Margaret J., and George S. McClellan. *Budgets and Financial Management in Higher Education.* San Francisco: Jossey-Bass, 2011.

Budd, John M. *The Changing Academic Library: Operations, Culture, Environments,* 2nd ed. Chicago: Association of College and Research Libraries, 2012.

"Budgeting & Finance." American Library Association. www.ala.org/tools/atoz/librarybudgetfinance/budgetfinance.

Dowell, David R, "Budgeting: Moving from Planning to Action." In *It's All About Student Learning. Managing Community and Other College Libraries in the 21st Century,* edited by David R. Dowell and Gerard B. McCabe. Westport, CT: Libraries Unlimited, 2006.

Lenker, Mark, and Elizabeth Kocevar-Weidinger. "Nonaffiliated Users in Academic Libraries: Using W.D. Ross's Ethical Pluralism to Make Sense of the Tough Questions." *College & Research Libraries* 71, no. 5 (September 2010): 421–434.

"Library Fund Raising: A Selected Annotated Bibliography. ALA Library Fact Sheet 24." Chicago: American Library Association. www.ala.org/tools/libfactsheets/alalibraryfactsheet24.

Regazzi, John J. "Constrained?—An Analysis of U.S. Academic Library Shifts in Spending, Staffing, and Utilization, 1998–2008. *College & Research Libraries* 73, no. 5 (September 2012): 449–468.

Thompson, Ronelle, and Ann M. Smith, compilers. *Friends of College Libraries*, 2nd ed.: CLIP Note # 27. Chicago: Association of College and Research Libraries, 1999.

23
Librarians Who Teach

Professional Identity As Educators

ASSERTION

An academic library administrator sees the professional identity of most librarians as educators, and continually provides ways and encouragement for those librarians to contribute as effective teachers.

COMMENTARY

Librarians Teach Groups

Most librarians have job duties that make them educators, whether they teach an individual or a group of students, in person or online. Academic library administrators should do as much as they can to promote and support librarians in this educator role. This is important for the ongoing role of librarians as teachers of information literacy, and, where appropriate, for evaluation and promotion as faculty.

The ability to teach a class of students is an important part of the criteria for hiring most librarians. These librarians will spend some of their time teaching information literacy to a group of students, especially those librarians organized in a liaison model and responsible for certain academic departments. Teaching a group of students usually means teaching face-to-face in a classroom, but it also means being embedded in course management software, or creating web-based tutorials.

Pedagogy

To be asked by classroom faculty to teach their students, librarians need to be willing and open to watching, learning, and incorporating effective teaching strategies for different conditions. Being recognized as effective teachers will likely result in requests for more teaching. Conversely, ordinary pedagogy and content will lead to fewer invitations, and less of a role for librarians in the educational process. Librarians ought to be recognized on campus as leading advocates of how to teach well, especially using flexible teaching space, active learning techniques, and instructional technology. This applies to instruction in classrooms, and when embedded in course management software. The role of library administrators is to encourage and support the development of the librarians so that they are recognized as outstanding teachers.

The Curriculum

If librarians have a teaching role, then they need to be clear with the instructor of a class about the content of what they can teach, that it is integrated into a class, and is not self-evident to most undergraduate or graduate students. The librarian contribution is not an "add on," but should be designed with the instructor to be part of the curriculum of a specific course. Many undergraduates have a limited background in understanding:

- how to ask the right questions (process),
- where to search (too much information "out there"), and
- how to find appropriate information (specialized knowledge).

What students at all levels can learn from effective information literacy instruction is how to ask the right questions, search effectively, and where to search for scholarly and vetted information. At some institutions, librarians teach a whole course on those topics.

A library administrator's role is to make sure that a process is in place to support and evaluate library instruction. The librarians need to think about their instructional role, collect and use data about their teaching, talk with classroom faculty about content and pedagogy, watch how the best instructors teach, and be open to new curricular units and ways of teaching.

Virtual Teaching

Librarians teach virtually when helping students through telephone, e-mail, chat, or text messages and conversations. Virtual teaching especially refers to when a librarian is embedded in a course (through course management software), and where there are links to content, tutorials, and to the librarian for guidance. A librarian can be embedded in online courses, and in blended or hybrid courses taught on campus. These feature a combination of face-to-face teaching and course management software.

APPLICATION

Teaching Spaces

There are often several different-sized spaces available within a library for information literacy instruction, but the instruction doesn't have to occur in the library. Depending on the size and needs of the class, space which can easily be changed has:

- high-speed wireless access,
- tables and chairs on wheels,
- walls, whiteboards, or glass boards for students to write on, and
- projection or digital screens.

If students have laptops, smartphones, or tablets, and if the librarian's content is web-based, then good teaching space can be just about anywhere, including in classrooms outside of the library. Wired computers do not have to define the space. Librarians who teach information literacy to groups of students ought to start their lesson planning with questions of content and effective pedagogy, and then find a space with the necessary attributes. One implication for academic library administrators is that the library teaching space may need remodeling into a space which can be easily changed, depending on the size and needs of a class.

Librarians Teach Through Reference/Research

Librarians teach individual students, most commonly through reference services. Reference services are one aspect of the larger research process. There are implications for administrators, especially as reference services have changed.

- The physical space where a reference/research conversation occurs may be at smaller desks in open areas, with movable monitors seen by both librarian and student.

- The reference book section is now significantly smaller than a decade (or more) ago.
- The reference/research conversation may occur in librarian offices. In addition to movable monitors, the participants might use their laptops or tablets.
- Virtual reference/research transactions may occur between students and a librarian embedded in course management software.
- Many reference/research conversations are not face-to-face, and instead consist of a tweet, chat, e-mail, or phone call.
- Some libraries use trained students at a Reference Desk, or they belong to a reference consortium.

The implications for administrators range from physically altering the reference area, to devoting time and money toward training staff in good practices for these individual reference conversations, whether online or in person. An administrator may also want data collected on reference transactions to understand what is actually occurring, and how best to staff reference services.

Improving Pedagogy

How do librarians stay current with good teaching strategies? Administrators can advocate for some practical strategies. Most colleges and universities have teacher training programs for students, instructional technology services for faculty, and a group to promote quality teaching by faculty. Librarians ought to learn actively from and participate in these groups. Library administrators might invite faculty from teacher training programs to present at staff development workshops. Librarians should be encouraged to seek out faculty as colleagues and allies who are involved in teacher preparation. There are often funds available for collaborative professional development, and partnering with faculty in the teacher training programs may raise the librarian's knowledge of research on teaching and learning.

Curriculum

It is desirable to have an information literacy page on the library's website. This is the place to link to ACRL standards, and to explain what librarians teach and how. Included should be web-based video tutorials. Another way to make the information literacy curriculum evident is to put a very large poster or two outlining the information literacy curriculum in the room or rooms where teaching occurs. The "curriculum on the wall" makes a statement to all those faculty and students who don't intuitively understand that there actually is an information literacy curriculum.

Instructional Choices

It is wise to offer choices to faculty about the content a librarian can teach, and then defer to the faculty member's judgment. Good co-teaching needs co-planning ahead of time. Using a checklist is helpful. The administrative role is to help the librarians build a consensus about talking ahead of time with faculty about what to teach, and an understanding among the librarians to share those best practices and best approaches.

Access Entitlement Principle

Academic librarians work with students online, and administrators should support the needs of librarians to effectively do that. The "Standards for Distance Learning Library Services" (Association of College and Research Libraries) refers to the "access entitlement principle." By definition each person who is a "member of an institution of higher education, is entitled to the library services and resources of that institution . . ." What does that mean in practice?

Course management system. Course management software contains the syllabus, readings, lectures, and a variety of links to content. Some librarians are "embedded" in course management software, and so can help students with research projects. The questions here are about the librarian being accepted by the instructor and students, the librarian's workload, and the use of effective techniques.

Distance learning. In distance courses the librarian may be embedded in the course management software. The questions for the library are about access for distance students to materials and librarian time. While most of the course content is electronic, a student may still need physical books, journal articles, or media. The student is paying for a course, and so the library has an obligation to provide physical materials as if the student was able to enter the library. It is not satisfactory to tell a student to find a local library and use it. Rather, the student needs online access to the librarians of the school to which tuition is paid, and journal articles and books. This is going to cost the library some money, and hence needs some procedural language and budget planning. Similar questions pertain to students in a study abroad course.

Assessment of Teaching

Librarians should assess the quality and effectiveness of their information literacy teaching, however it is defined, and whether or not librarians are faculty. Administrators and librarians need to use that positive or negative data for continuous reflection and improvement, and to demonstrate the instructional role of librarians and curriculum in learning outcomes for students.

A good way to assess librarian teaching is to first work with someone in the institution's office that collects data about the quality of teaching. There may be existing ways to assess teaching, especially in the research process, and especially if connected to student learning outcomes. Develop a plan for what data the librarians should collect, and how to integrate it with other data collected about students and teaching. The librarians might capture data after teaching a session, or after collaborating with faculty on a course. Some of this could be correlated with other data collected in an academic discipline over the college career of individuals.

Unobtrusively collecting data takes the time and interest of librarians, and the willingness of the course instructor. The administrator's role is to make sure that data collection is defined, occurs in reliable and valid ways, and is considered part of a teaching librarian's work. Then someone needs to correlate, analyze, and understand it. The final part is knowing what to share, with whom, and when.

Seniors

Seniors in many institutions do a capstone project or a thesis. It is really helpful if the faculty member builds into the process an individual meeting between the student and a librarian who has subject knowledge in that area. Graduate students writing a thesis or dissertation should also be connected to a librarian with the subject knowledge. Some libraries put these senior theses, or all the graduate theses and dissertations, on special shelving or an Institutional Repository and are proud of the accumulated record.

READING

STANDARDS AND GUIDELINES

American Association of Community Colleges. "AACC Position Statement on Information Literacy." Washington, DC: American Association of Community Colleges, 2008. www.aacc.nche.edu/About/Positions/Pages/ps05052008.aspx.

Association of College and Research Libraries. "Characteristics of Programs of Information Literacy that Illustrate Best Practices: A Guideline." Chicago:

Association of College and Research Libraries, 2012. www.ala.org/acrl/standards/characteristics.

Association of College and Research Libraries. "Guidelines for Instruction Programs in Academic Libraries." Chicago: Association of College and Research Libraries, 2011. www.ala.org/acrl/standards/guidelinesinstruction.

Association of College and Research Libraries. "Information Literacy Competency Standards for Higher Education." Chicago: Association of College and Research Libraries, 2000. www.ala.org/acrl/standards/informationliteracycompetency.

Association of College and Research Libraries. "Information Literacy Competency Standards Toolkit." Chicago: Association of College and Research Libraries. www.ala.org/acrl/issues/infolit/standards/standardstoolkit.

Association of College and Research Libraries. "Information Literacy Resources." Chicago: Association of College and Research Libraries. www.ala.org/acrl/issues/infolit.

Association of College and Research Libraries. "Standards for Distance Learning Library Services." Chicago: Association of College and Research Libraries, 2008. www.ala.org/acrl/standards/guidelinesdistancelearning.

Association of College and Research Libraries. "Standards for Libraries in Higher Education." Chicago: American Library Association, 2011. www.ala.org/acrl/standards/standardslibraries.

Association of College and Research Libraries. "Standards for Proficiencies for Instruction Librarians and Coordinators." Chicago: Association of College and Research Libraries, 2007. www.ala.org/acrl/standards/profstandards.

ADVICE AND RESEARCH

Alire, Camila A., and G. Edward Evans. *Academic Librarianship*. New York: Neal-Schuman Publishers, Inc., 2010.

Balcziunas, Adam, and Larissa Gordon. "Walking a Mile in Their Shoes: Librarians As Teaching Faculty." *College & Research Libraries News* (April 2012): 192–195.

Blevens, Cheryl L. "Catching Up with Information Literacy Assessment: Resources for Program Evaluation." *College & Research Libraries News* 73, no. 4 (April 2012): 202–206.

Hall, Russell A. "Beyond the Job Ad: Employers and Library Instruction." *College & Research Libraries* 74, no. 1 (January 2013): 24–38.

Head, Alison, and Michael Eisenberg. "Project Information Literacy: A Large-Scale Study about Early Adults and Their Research Habits." http://projectinfolit.org.

Hook, Sheril. "Impact? What Three Years of Research Tell Us about Library Instruction." *College & Research Libraries News* 73, no. 1 (January 2012): 7–10.

Kemp, Jane. "Isn't Being a Librarian Enough? Librarians As Classroom Teachers." *College and Undergraduate Libraries* 13, no. 3 (2006): 3–23.

Kvenild, Cassandra, and Kaijsa Calkins, eds. *Embedded Librarians: Moving Beyond One-Shot Instruction.* Chicago: American Library Association, 2011.

Long, Matthew P., and Roger C. Schonfeld. "Ithaka S+R Library Survey 2010: Insights from U.S. Academic Library Directors," 2011. www.sr.ithaka.org/research-publications/library-survey-2010.

McAdoo, Monty L. *Building Bridges: Connecting Faculty, Students, and the College Library.* Chicago, IL: American Library Association, 2010.

McAdoo, Monty L. *Fundamentals of Library Instruction.* Chicago: American Library Association, 2012.

McGuiness, Claire. *Becoming Confident Teachers: A Guide for Academic Librarians.* Oxford: Chandos Publishing, 2011.

Radcliff, Carolyn J., Mary Lee Jensen, Joseph A. Salem, Jr., Kenneth J. Burhanna, and Julie A. Gedeon. *A Practical Guide to Information Literacy Assessment for Academic Librarians.* Westport, CT: Libraries Unlimited, 2007.

Radford, Marie L. and Lorri M. Mon. "Reference Service in Face-to-Face and Virtual Environments." In *Academic Library Research: Perspectives and Current Trends* edited by Marie L. Radford and Pamela Snelson. Chicago: Association of College and Research Libraries, 2008.

Shumaker, David. *The Embedded Librarian: Innovative Strategies for Taking Knowledge Where It's Needed.* Medford, NJ: Information Today, Inc., 2012.

Steiner, Sarah K., and M. Leslie Madden, eds. *The Desk and Beyond: Next Generation Reference Services.* Chicago: Association of College and Research Libraries, 2008.

24
Building

Designed for Teaching, Learning, and Technology

ASSERTION

The academic library Director advocates for rearranging or remodeling the library space in order for the library building to remain a foundational part of the institution's educational agenda.

COMMENTARY

Use of Library Space

When changes in teaching, learning, and technology make it clear that some of the library space needs to be used differently, then the academic library Director needs to initiate and stay involved in a project to make building changes. If there is space in the library that is perceived as underused, then that space will inevitably attract non-library proposals for using it. In academic institutions that are short of space, someone may assign a non-library function into space that is perceived to be underused. Office space or programs that aren't part of the definition of the library, and with staff who don't report to the library Director, will potentially change the library into a multi-purpose building. It is hard to reclaim space in a multi-purpose building for purposes defined as "library" or under the management of the library Director. That is why it is important for the Director to not be passive about the uses of library space. The Director and staff need to actively try to keep spaces used, with a definition of their purposes on the library website. Or, the Director needs to initiate a process leading to the remodel and reuse of some aspect of the library.

Learning Commons

A definition of some of the library building's space as a "learning commons" raises the questions of what activities should be under the library's physical roof, and under the library's governance structure. If services for students such as writing, tutoring, and computer assistance are in the library building, then the definition of this library needs to clearly include such activities. In that case, the term "library" needs an expansive definition that includes these learning services. If, however, such services are tenants in reconfigured library space, and are not integrated into the overall definition and governance of the library, then there will probably be ongoing issues over governance, space, and budget. Such a situation also makes it harder to redefine the library (both space and librarian job definitions) because there is history in the way. If the library and learning commons functions are within one building, and under the governance of the library Director, then the definition of the library can be expanded to include those learning commons services, and change with student needs and technology.

Facilities Department

The relationship between the library Director and key people in the Facilities department is important. One group in Facilities is responsible for custodial and maintenance needs, and another for capital projects. It is important to the image of the library that the custodial and maintenance group keeps the library building clean, free of graffiti, and repaired. It is also important that the capital project leaders believe in the worth and value of an effective library building. They need to see the value to the institution of expensive capital projects in the library, ranging from a substantial remodeling, to new wiring, HVAC, carpet, or furniture. They may also be interested in a "greener" library building, which pays attention to various levels of Leadership in Energy and Environmental Design (LEED) standards. All of this starts with the history and current relationship between the library Director and the decision-makers in Facilities.

Replacement Cycle

Library buildings and their furnishings need scheduled renewal. Taking care of ongoing maintenance, such as cleaning, painting, and repair, is usually the responsibility of the Facilities department. The Facilities department usually pays for replacement of larger capital items, such as carpet and furniture, and systems (e.g., wiring and HVAC). The Director needs to understand what items are paid from the library budget, and what items are paid from other campus funds, and the process by which those decisions are made. The Director is a steward of the library building. As such, the Director needs to know how to get a capital library project in line for approval, and what can be done to move along the library project.

Food and Drink

Patrons should be able to eat and drink in the library: academic library administrators and library staff should no longer worry about it. The library's response should be to provide plenty of visible trash and recycle containers, and take down signs prohibiting food and drink. Trust the students to be respectful of the privilege of having beverages and snacks at library tables and carrels. Most students assume that they can have snacks and beverages in the library. Commuting and graduate students really appreciate it. By having no signs about food and drink, administrators and staff have changed the image of the library from "We are worried about what you might do" to "Welcome, this is your place and we trust you to use it respectfully."

Discard

It hurts the library image to have outdated technology (e.g., record players and VHS machines), or content in unused formats (e.g., print indices which are now online) taking up visible space, especially if not considered useful for academic research. Seeing outdated technology and formats creates an image of the library as a place that stores things that nobody uses. The Director should always be aware of the library's image, and whether or not the image is compromised because under-used items are publicly visible. For example, if an old format such as vinyl records has value, then those items should be sold or, if worth keeping, then moved into less visible or closed storage.

APPLICATION

Inexpensive Changes

Some changes in the library building can be made at little or moderate cost, and academic library administrators should advocate for such. One example is rearranging space. Before moving things around, it is wise to establish some guidelines for rearranging space. For example, a guideline might be that people prefer to sit by windows (hence, move tables and chairs to windows), and objects should be stored in windowless areas (hence, move shelving into windowless areas). It is smart to establish guidelines, measure, use a CAD program, and evaluate those plans before moving anything. Other inexpensive changes that can change interior spaces are paint colors, improved lighting, and a considerable number of large indoor plants. A really helpful activity is to reevaluate signage and improve it where needed.

Moderately Expensive Changes

Some changes are moderately expensive, and the academic library Director should advocate for them, because they can have a positive impact on the staff and student perception of the library. For example, multiple (and relatively unobtrusive) security gates at the entrance can make a better initial impression than funneling patrons through one gate. The use of high-end systems furniture pieces can notably define work spaces. New flooring in one or two high-traffic areas can be helpful. Dingy bathrooms can be updated. Large display screens throughout high-traffic areas change the perception of the library. There are a number of changes that will contribute toward a "greener" library building, starting with energy and water conservation. These and other moderately expensive changes can make an impact on how the building is perceived and treated by library staff and the campus community.

Student Advice

The institution may have a degree program in interior design, architecture, or art. If so, there may be a way for administrators to engage a class in studying some aspect of improving the library space. Or, administrators may employ a few students as interns to give advice or guidelines for the arrangement of the interior of the library. It is useful to have a set of "as built" plans of floors and areas. These are necessary when considering any rearrangement. If the Facilities department doesn't have useful "as builts," then students can measure the space and produce CAD drawings for future use.

Student advice about the library can be obtained through focus groups. The question always is how to gather enough students to obtain a valid and reliable sample. Sometimes working with student government leaders can lead to student participation. So will offering gift cards.

Displays and Exhibits

If there is suitable space, then the library should display and exhibit art (and especially student art and class projects), travelling exhibits, and archival material. It is wise to have a library policy on displays and exhibits. That policy should be nested within the institutional policy on displays and exhibits (and on donated art), vetted by top administrators, have forms to sign, and be posted on the library website. Decisions about what to display, where, and the length of the exhibit should be made by library staff. Without a policy on displays and exhibits, then pieces of art and displays not connected to the library can end up there, sometimes with awkward consequences. Questions of liability and vandalism also need to be addressed.

At the end of a term, classes often need a place to display posters or art projects. It is very good for the library to make space available for student projects. It injects some new visual life into the library. It also brings in students and their friends to look at what they made. It is wise to work with faculty before the term begins about the details, so that students know they are making projects to go on display, and everyone is clear about where the work will go and for how long. Share the library policy on displays and exhibits with students, so they know that decisions about content, location, and duration are made by the library staff. The library might also buy student art for its display collection.

In addition to displaying art, student work, and exhibits, the library should also display announcements about the library, and campus events. To do that, the library needs large flat screens in multiple locations. Usually the announcements list the library's schedule for that day, upcoming events, and advertisements for library services.

Be a Building Supervisor

The Director and other administrators in an academic library need to act like building supervisors. They need the ability to open and lock doors, knowledge of how to turn on and off the lights and the alarms, knowledge of what happens when the electricity fails, and the location of everything from wiring closets to plumbing. The administrator isn't replacing anyone in charge of those tasks. Rather, when it is necessary or expected, being able to unlock doors, shut off an alarm, or know where things are located is useful. Each administrator also needs to know the layout of the building in some detail. When the police enter during an emergency and turn to the administrator and ask for the location of all exits, then it is important to know well the design of the building.

Entering the Library

When administrators enter and exit the building, they should walk through the front entrance rather than coming in a side employee entrance. That way they can exchange greetings with those working at the main desk. Additionally, the administrator will notice how the place looks from the perspective of patrons entering the library. Is anything amiss, especially first thing in the morning? While entering and exiting during the day, is the first impression still positive? And there is always the question of signage, and whether it is quickly evident which direction to walk.

Furniture

Administrators need to see that broken or worn-out furniture is removed from view. Keeping sub-standard furnishings sends the message that the people in charge are either too poor to take action, or their standards are too low. Duct tape covering worn-out chair cushions or carpet sends an inexcusable message to students and faculty, which can be generalized to other aspects of the library. The Director is accountable for the appearance of the library, and when things are broken or worn out, they need to be removed or replaced because their continued existence raises doubts about the library, the Director, and other leaders in the institution.

Fix It

Even in the best libraries, graffiti and vandalism inevitably occur, and sometimes things are "out of order." In well-managed libraries, administrators see that such problems are attended to promptly. Graffiti must be removed within the day. Computers that don't work need something other than a handwritten "out of order" sign taped over the screen. A better solution is to print some signs, inform the reader that the problem is being taken care of, include library contact information, indicate the date when the problem occurred, and use these signs right away. Anything in a building which is broken, worn out, or the object of graffiti, and not attended to in a prompt manner, lowers respect for that building and invites disrespect.

Bathrooms

Administrators ought to intentionally use different bathrooms in the library throughout the day, and encourage staff to do likewise. As those who are accountable, and responsible for quality control, administrators need to know if there are problems with dirty conditions, graffiti, or the plumbing. Some bathrooms are likely used far more than the assumptions in the cleaning and restocking schedule. Obtain some data in order to propose a maintenance solution. Be clear with all library staff that they need to report bathroom issues right away. Clean, maintained bathrooms that are easy to locate are really important for the library's positive image.

Reporting

Centralize in one library staff member all requests for maintenance. If requests aren't reported by one person, then the library loses credibility with staff in the Facilities department. If one person reports and tracks that work order, then a better connection between the library and some workers in Facilities will be made. If work issues are reported by the Administrative Assistant, then the Director (or another administrator) will know when something has been reported, the timeline for attention, and if it is being fixed promptly. That is when the Director may need to "climb the ladder" in order to get something done, although complaining to supervisors should be done rarely, and only when necessary.

Moving Furniture

Students move around the library tables and chairs, and open and close window blinds. Administrators and the staff members who close and open the library should agree that each morning the furniture should be back where staff think it belongs, not where some students rearranged it the previous night for their study sessions. Usually that means that library staff or student employees who closed at night, or opened in the morning, should walk through the library and make sure that furnishings are back to "normal."

Noise

There are always students who don't understand the library's contextual clues about where talking is and is not appropriate. Subtle clues are better than too many "No Talking" signs. A floor or area of the library can be designated for quiet study. Sometimes furniture helps define quiet areas. Individual tables with one chair and a desk lamp set a tone for quiet study. Tables with six chairs indicate "OK to talk." Furniture, lighting, and "tradition" are as effective as signs. If library staff encounter inappropriate talking that is bothering others, then the staff member should introduce him or herself, remind the students that some parts of the library are for group work, and some for quiet study, and offer to find that group a study room where talking doesn't bother others.

READING

STANDARDS AND GUIDELINES

Association of College and Research Libraries. "Standards for Libraries in Higher Education." Chicago: American Library Association, 2011. www.ala.org/acrl/standards/standardslibraries.

ADVICE AND RESEARCH

Alire, Camila A., and G. Edward Evans. *Academic Librarianship*. New York: Neal-Schuman Publishers, Inc., 2010.

Association of College and Research Libraries (ACRL) and the Library Leadership and Management Association (LLAMA). "Academic Library Building Design: Resources for Planning." Chicago: American Library Association. http://wikis.ala.org/acrl/index.php/ACRL/LLAMA_Guide_for_Architects_and_Librarians#Academic_Library_Building_Design:_Resources_for_Planning.

Barclay, Donald, and Eric Scott. "Directions to Library Wayfinding." *American Libraries*. March/April 2012. http://americanlibrariesmagazine.org/features/03202012/directions-library-wayfinding.

Barclay, Donald A., and Eric D. Scott. *The Library Renovation, Maintenance, and Construction Handbook*. New York: Neal-Schuman Publishers, Inc., 2011.

Bennett, Scott. "Learning Behaviors and Learning Spaces." *portal: Libraries and the Academy*. 11, no. 3 (July 2011): 765–789.

"Building Libraries and Library Additions: A Selected Annotated Bibliography." ALA Library Fact Sheet 11. Chicago: American Library Association. www.ala.org/tools/libfactsheets/alalibraryfactsheet11.

Fortriede, Steven Carl. *Moving Your Library. Getting the Collection from Here to There.* Chicago: American Library Association, 2010.

Freeman, Geoffrey T., Scott Bennett, Sam Demas, Bernard Frischer, Christina A. Peterson, and Kathleen Burr Oliver. *Library as Place: Rethinking Roles, Rethinking Space*. Washington, DC: Council on Library and Information Resources, 2005.

"Green Libraries: A Website for Information about Green and Sustainable Libraries." http://greenlibraries.org.

Habich, Elizabeth Chamberlain. *Moving Library Collections: A Management Handbook*, 2nd ed. Santa Barbara, CA: Libraries Unlimited, 2010.

Kemp, Jane, and Witschi, Laura, compilers "Displays and Exhibits in College Libraries: CLIP Note # 25." Chicago: Association of College and Research Libraries, 1997.

Mash, S. David. *Decision-Making in the Absence of Certainty: A Study in the Context of*

Technology and the Construction of the 21st Century Academic Library. Chicago: American Library Association, 2011.

Mitchell, Eleanor. "Place Planning for Libraries: The Space Near the Heart of the College." In *Defining Relevancy: Managing the New Academic Library*, edited by Janet McNeil Hurlbert. Westport, CT: Libraries Unlimited, 2008.

"Participatory Design in Academic Libraries: Methods, Findings, and Implementations." Washington, DC: Council on Library and Information Resources, 2012.

Planning Academic and Research Library Buildings, 3rd ed. Chicago: American Library Association, 2000.

Sannwald, William W. *Checklist of Library Building Design Considerations,* 5th Edition. Chicago: American Library Association, 2009.

Stewart, Christopher. *The Academic Library Building in the Digital Age: A Study of Construction, Planning, and Design of New Library Space.* Chicago: Association of College and Research Libraries, 2010.

Woodward, Jeannette. *Creating the Customer-Driven Academic Library.* Chicago: American Library Association, 2009.

25
Collections

Meeting High Expectations for Content

ASSERTION

The academic library Director advocates for the library being in a consortium of academic libraries with a shared consortial collection.

COMMENTARY

Consortia

There is neither enough money nor enough space to acquire and store the intellectual content that faculty and students expect from an academic library. Faculty earned their PhDs at research institutions with impressive libraries, and expect to keep reading, researching, and writing in specialized fields, even if the library where they now work is much smaller. Consequently, to meet expectations for content, all academic libraries are more effective when part of a consortium (or several consortia). Even large, well-funded libraries become better when part of a consortium. Within consortia the individual libraries should be able to increase access to content by being able to:

- exchange materials, and
- develop collections as consortial collections.

Additionally, members of a consortium can usually:

- lower the price of contracts for electronic resources because of the group's buying power,
- share technical services (e.g., specialized cataloging),
- host as much electronic content as possible at web scale instead of hosting and maintaining it locally,
- apply for and have a higher chance of receiving grants,
- provide some consortial services at the level provided by the best libraries in the consortium (e.g., a consortial Institutional Repository or consortial archival assistance), and
- provide professional learning and collegiality for those library staff involved in the work of the consortium.

Cost

Being part of a content-sharing consortium does not necessarily lower the operational costs of the library. Consortial purchasing might lower the costs of some contracts, and reduce the staff FTE assigned to tasks which no longer need to be done locally. However, there is also a cost to membership, ranging from consortial staff and courier service to systems software. Between institutional and library budgets, the Provost and academic library Director need to rearrange allocations in order to be an ongoing member of a consortium. A consortial library increases access to content and recalibrates what students and faculty expect from a library. Turning the ratchet back to being an isolated library seems inconceivable.

Collection Management Document

An administrator needs to see that a policy and procedures Collection Management document is written and used. It should describe the life cycle of all library intellectual content. It is the job of the librarians to choose (and withdraw) the content, based on what they know of the curriculum and research in their institution. The overall Collection Management document identifies the process used for decisions. If the library belongs to a consortium, then this document will be written from that perspective.

Collection Priorities

If an academic library is part of a consortium, and supplements that with an Inter-Library Loan program, then collection development consists of three descending priorities:

- supporting the institution's library-using curriculum,
- buying titles which are expected in the library of an academic institution of this size, and
- supporting the distinctive attributes of this college or university.

The library doesn't have to own a wide variety of content, but rather own in these three areas and then be able to borrow the rest through a consortium or Inter-Library Loan. This allows librarians to define and collect in areas which are of special local interest, derived from institutional identity and strong departments. Collection development begins with the best data from librarians about what is needed and will be used within this institution. Collecting in local areas of strength also contributes to the consortial collection. A consortial agreement may define how many total copies of one title should be in the aggregated collection. Or, a consortium may create a distributed print repository, through which designated libraries keep under-used titles, and the other libraries discard those titles.

Collection Analysis

Analyzing a book collection in terms of what is held and used will differ depending on membership in a consortium. A collection's database may be compared to external standards and guidelines, or against the collection of another institution. That can be useful on one level in showing strengths and gaps. However, it takes knowledge of the curriculum and research at an institution in order to know how well-aligned the collection is with those educational needs. If part of a consortium, then the ability to share titles makes collection analysis against external standards less helpful. What matters is if the library provides in a timely manner the content that faculty and students need.

Right Content in the Right Format, Right Now

Faculty and students want quick access to the right content. If the library does not provide access to the desired content, or if the content is there but the process for obtaining it is too cumbersome and slow, then those patrons will work around the library and look elsewhere. Getting the right content in the right format to faculty and students, department by department, and within their timeframe, is politically essential for the ongoing budgetary support of the library. The Director should talk with librarians about faculty and student usage of content (local and consortial), be aware of when usage is waning, and then do something about it. Can the budget priorities be rearranged to subscribe to the electronic version of what some faculty say they will use? Is there usage data to show disappointed faculty when the library drops something with low usage in order to buy or subscribe to something else of a perceived higher value?

Reference Collection

Many academic libraries were designed with large, prominent spaces for a Reference collection. As web-based reference content has replaced reference books, many libraries have significantly remodeled that space, and reduced the size of the Reference print collection. It is expensive to move reference content from print to electronic format, the packaging isn't always equivalent, and there is still a need for some print reference works. However, the size and space of the Reference collection need to be reevaluated continually. Such space is usually of high visibility, and hence should have high use. If the current Reference collection isn't the highest use of that space, then the administrator needs to start a process which reconsiders all aspects of Reference, starting with definitions.

Systems Software

To be part of one or more consortia, the library may need to operate the right systems software so that material can be identified, checked out, and returned throughout a consortial system. Licensing systems software is expensive. It is usually politically hard within an institution to obtain more funds for a new and more expensive software solution. If a library chooses one system, but in retrospect should have chosen another to be in a consortium, then a new request for additional funds is politically awkward. The cost to changing systems software is in licensing fees, administration of the system, and staff training. If being in a consortium is a priority, then that will drive the choice of systems software.

Cataloging

The rules and procedures which define how academic libraries describe their intellectual resources (so that resources can be found) are shifting from Anglo-American Cataloguing Rules, Second Edition (AACR2), which originated before digital content, to RDA, "Resource Description and Access." RDA is a set of rules used for making bibliographic records designed to better describe digital content than AACR2. A Director should rely on the judgment of the library's head cataloger about the implications for the library of MARC catalog records made in RDA.

Intellectual Freedom

Requests that are outside the Collection Management guidelines to buy, not buy, or remove any library content are rare in academic libraries. However, when it happens, it will likely be a test of the Director's leadership. The librarians and the library need to be protected through the written, vetted, and signed Collection Management document, which should be posted on the library website. The relevant parts are how library content is selected, and the procedure for reconsideration, including clarity about decision-making authority for removal. All requests which deal with intellectual freedom need to be taken seriously because it is impossible to predict how a request can escalate. If librarians have strong opinions about the request, if the campus media get involved, or if there is external pressure from donors on campus administrators, then an intellectual freedom challenge can have consequences for the Director's leadership.

Institutional Repository

Some libraries will create and manage an Institutional Repository (IR) for their students and faculty, or arrange for the use of an IR within a consortium. An IR becomes a "collection" within the library. It is where students and faculty can store papers, theses, dissertations, or other projects, and know that their material may be safely accessed under defined conditions. Providing and maintaining an IR is usually a service of value provided by the library to the campus community. It comes at a cost to the library in terms of software, staff time, and budget, so it must be capable of being sustained.

Special Collections

Sometimes an academic library can justify having a "special" collection. The threshold for making a special collection should be high. It is often connected in some way to institutional identity. The library should try to collect more deeply on this topic than otherwise. There may be additional funding, such as an endowment, to support this collection. A special collection may have its own location, or it may be shelved with the general collection (but accessed by using descriptive terms).

Archives and Records Management

The library needs to be responsible for collecting the institution's records and managing its archives. An archivist knows how to acquire, catalog, preserve, and make available the physical and electronic content in the institution's archives. Archival content is similar to other intellectual content held by the library, and used by patrons of the library. The acquisition and use of archival content has legal implications, and archivists are careful about procedures and permissions. Especially in smaller colleges and universities, the library Director needs to demonstrate to top administrators that the archives should be under the jurisdiction of the library, even if the collection is stored elsewhere.

Library involvement in archives and institutional records management has a serious price tag, starting with salaries. There is an escalating need for physical and server space. The Director and archivist need to define (and limit) what the library can realistically collect based on the institution's funding for staff and storage space. One part of that is deciding what to collect outside of institutional records. The other part is setting guidelines for departments within the institution. If the institution has not spent enough money to do records management and archives adequately, then the library Director needs to lower the expectations, and define what is fiscally prudent and necessary to do. That usually means working with the Information Technology group, and perhaps the leaders of several other departments (e.g., Trustees, President's Office, Budget, Registrar, Facilities, and Advancement) to establish campus-wide guidelines and procedures for all departments to take care of their own records.

APPLICATION

Departmental Collection Management Document

It is desirable to have specific department-level Collection Management documents which outline the library priorities for that department. These should be made and maintained by librarians, working with faculty from these departments. This is how library-using faculty can give specific guidelines for what they want librarians to purchase, starting with the ratio between books, journals, and media. The librarians will know how to implement these guidelines with specific titles and packages. Every three to five years these department-level documents should be renewed.

Curriculum Map

How do librarians know what is actually being taught in each department, and what to buy to support the curriculum? One way is to obtain syllabi and make a curriculum map. Working with a departmental Administrative Assistant, liaison librarians can normally obtain electronic copies of syllabi. Then librarians can chart the topics taught in each course. This is good to update every few years, and look for patterns that might otherwise be overlooked.

Faculty

A librarian with collection management responsibility for a subject area needs to know what is actually being taught in a department (e.g., review syllabi), what faculty and students are researching (e.g., communicate with them), and the journal literature (e.g., skim articles and read reviews). The academic library administrator's responsibility is to see that librarians buy content based on knowledge from doing the above. Librarians can forward book reviews to faculty, but a better understanding comes from knowing the curriculum and research interests in a department, and then buying accordingly. That is why a liaison model is helpful for collection development, and why librarians ought to attend faculty meetings in their areas of responsibility, and be on the internal faculty e-mail lists for those areas. It is very desirable if a liaison librarian is given faculty status in a department, school, or college because that provides access.

Gifts

Encouraging gifts of money and materials is one small way to grow the collections. Librarians should intentionally identify and talk with certain faculty prior to retirement and request a donation of their books, papers, or other items when they are ready. Gifts of materials should be welcomed from anyone, rather than being viewed as a sign of weakness ("Our library is so poor that we need to take gifts of used books"). Gifts of books should not be viewed as a nuisance that causes extra work and is of limited benefit. One never knows how a donation might lead to another, and to subsequent items of real value. Working with staff in the Advancement office may also lead to gifts of money and materials, especially if library staff can provide a list of desired items.

Popular Fiction

There are students, faculty, and campus staff who read popular fiction. While public libraries are normally the place to obtain such titles, an academic library is convenient, and some members of the campus community will welcome popular fiction in the library. For a small annual investment, an academic library can provide best-selling popular fiction paperbacks or e-books. Library staff might be surprised by the interest in this collection, especially if titles are set apart and advertised. A collection of popular fiction fills a need and is effective public relations.

Withdrawing Items

The library Collection Management document should give guidelines for iden-tifying titles of items to remove. This is work best done by librarians when school is not in session. It is really helpful to have a faculty member look at part of a collection with the librarian. A faculty member could be compensated for his or her time, or have influence over what is next purchased in that area. Besides withdrawing titles based on guidelines, the library's consortium and the amount of shelving space in the library building are factors.

Withdrawing Paper Journals

Storing paper backfiles of journals requires shelving space, whether on tra-ditional or compact shelving. If those journals don't receive much use, then storing paper journals on traditional shelving may generate proposals from outside the library for discarding journals and reusing that space. A proac-tive academic library Director works with the library staff to make a plan before someone external to the library imposes a decision. There are two considerations:

1. How will the space be reused? Reusing space goes to the definition of the library. What is the line between the library including various learning services, and the library becoming a multi-purpose building?
2. How will the library provide electronic access to journal backfiles? Pro-viding backfile access to journals requires purchasing JSTOR modules, electronic backfile packages from the journal owners, knowing that the backfiles are included in another electronic package, or having consor-tial arrangements to the content. This is complex, and can change (e.g., a title can be dropped from an aggregated package). It may also not be important, unless managing a research library where access to back-files of journals is basic to the collection.

Withdrawing paper journals is an expensive project in terms of staff time, repurposing space, and (if needed) providing electronic access to backfiles (to replace what was discarded). There are some serious financial costs. There may also be a political cost from some faculty who want print journals retained. The Director needs to work with the Provost and Facilities and sign off on a detailed plan before starting.

Outdated Formats

What to do with material in formats which are rarely used, such as 16mm film, microforms, vinyl records, or VHS tapes? The first consideration is what such formats do to the image of the library. If such items are still in view, then they will create a negative perception of what the library is and what it has.

That perception will not just be among students (curious to scornful), but also among some faculty and campus administrators, who may wonder aloud why the library is using expensive space to store content in unused formats. The internal debate among librarians needs to determine if there is any value in keeping all or some of these items. If some are still used, or if they have historical value, then they need to be stored out of sight. That means transferring them to off-site storage, putting them in dark storage in the library, or even giving them away to a faculty member who uses them. The other option is to sell them, and put the money into the library endowment. Cleaning house is not optional, but is part of intentionally cultivating an image of the library as technologically sophisticated.

Disposal

Administrators need to be aware of how best to dispose of unwanted library items, maybe make some money in the process, and certainly avoid paying fees for disposal. State institutions have defined procedures for disposal of state property. Private institutions likely have procedures, but not as restrictive as state regulations. There are companies that take unwanted books and sell them online, or libraries sometimes have their own book sales. Before planning a sale, or paying to recycle or dump unwanted books (or other materials), check with the person charged with disposing of surplus property. There may be a business that will take these items, and send you a little money if some are sold online. An entrepreneurial administrator may find ways to make money from unwanted books, media, archival items, or library furniture. Be careful about where and how you discard library material. Putting library books in a campus dumpster seems simple and cheap, but, when noticed, may generate adverse publicity, starting with student journalists.

READING

STANDARDS AND GUIDELINES

American Library Association. "Interlibrary Loan Code for the United States." Chicago: American Library Association, 2008. www.ala.org/rusa/resources/guidelines/interlibrary.

Association of College and Research Libraries. "Guidelines on the Selection and Transfer of Materials from General Collections to Special Collections." Chicago: Association of College and Research Libraries, 2008. www.ala.org/acrl/standards/selctransfer.

Association of College and Research Libraries. "Standards for Libraries in Higher Education." Chicago: American Library Association, 2011. www.ala.org/acrl/standards/standardslibraries.

ADVICE AND RESEARCH

"ACRL/SAA Joint Statement on Access to Research Materials in Archives and Special Collections Libraries." Association of College and Research Libraries/Society of American Archivists. 2009. www.ala.org/acrl/standards/jointstatement.

Alire, Camila A., and G. Edward Evans. *Academic Librarianship*. New York: Neal-Schuman Publishers, Inc., 2010.

Budd, John M. *The Changing Academic Library: Operations, Culture, Environments*, 2nd ed. Chicago: Association of College and Research Libraries, 2012.

Curtis, Sharon K., Doralyn Rossman, and Molly C. A. Anderson. "Value-Based Return on Investment in the Entrepreneurial Disposition of Library Materials." In *The Entrepreneurial Librarian: Essays on the Infusion of Private-Business Dynamism into the Professional Service,* edited by Mary Krautter, Mary Beth Lock, and Mary G. Scanlon. Jefferson, NC: McFarland & Company, Inc., 2012.

Franks, Patricia C. *Records and Information Management*. Chicago: Neal-Schuman, an imprint of the American Library Association, 2013.

Gilbert, Julie and Barbara Fister. "Reading, Risk, and Reality: College Students and Reading for Pleasure." *College & Research Libraries* 72, no. 5 (September 2011): 474–495.

Johnson, Carol P., and Ann M. Keene. "Opportunities for Small and Medium-Sized College Archives in the Digital Age." In *Defining Relevancy: Managing the New Academic Library,* edited by Janet McNeil Hurlbert. Westport, CT: Libraries Unlimited, 2008.

Kelley, Steve. "What Is RDA, and Why Should E-book Managers Care?" In *No Shelf Required 2: Use and Management of Electronic Books,* edited by Sue Polanka. Chicago: American Library Association, 2012.

Lewis, David W. "From Stacks to the Web: The Transformation of Academic Library Collecting." *College & Research Libraries* 74, no. 2 (March 2013): 159–177.

Long, Matthew P., and Roger C. Schonfeld. "Ithaka S+R Library Survey 2010: Insights from U.S. Academic Library Directors," 2011. www.sr.ithaka.org/research-publications/library-survey-2010.

Manning, Mary, and Judy Silva. "Dual Archivist/Librarians: Balancing the Benefits and Challenges of Diverse Responsibilities." *College & Research Libraries* 73, no. 2 (March 2012): 164–181.

Mitchell, Eleanor, Peggy Seiden, and Suzy Taraba, eds. *Past or Portal? Enhancing Undergraduate Learning through Special Collections and Archives*. Chicago: Association of College and Research Libraries, 2012.

Purcell, Aaron D. *Academic Archives: Managing the Next Generation of College and University Archives, Records, and Special Collections*. Chicago: Neal-Schuman, 2012.

Singer, Carol A. *Fundamentals of Managing Reference Collections*. Chicago: American Library Association, 2012.

Society of American Archivists. www2.archivists.org.

Staley, David J. "Futures Thinking for Academic Librarians: Scenarios for the Future of the Book." Chicago: Association of College and Research Libraries, 2012. www.ala.org/acrl/sites/ala.org.acrl/files/content/issues/value/scenarios2012 .pdf.

Velucci, Sherry L. "Knowledge Organization." In *Academic Library Research. Perspectives and Current Trends,* edited by Marie L. Radford and Pamela Snelson. Chicago: Association of College and Research Libraries, 2008.

Video Round Table (VRT). Chicago: American Library Association. www.ala.org/vrt.

"Weeding Library Collections: A Selected Annotated Bibliography for Library Collection Evaluation, *ALA Library Fact Sheet 15.*" Chicago: American Library Association. www.ala.org/tools/libfactsheets/alalibraryfactsheet15.

Weible, Charie L., and Karen Janke, eds. *Interlibrary Loan Practices Handbook,* 3rd ed. Chicago: American Library Association, 2011.

26
Website and Social Media

Designed for Maximum Use

ASSERTION

The academic library Director is accountable for the design of the library website and related applications so that library electronic content is used as much and as easily as possible.

COMMENTARY

Creation and Control

There are usually standards, protocols, and templates that are defined by staff at some level in the college or university and used campus-wide for all websites, social media, and mobile applications. The library web staff will need to work with these people and within these campus parameters. There may be staff from multiple departments with responsibility for some aspect of campus websites. Hence, creating the library website will take some time and political skill. Various people from across campus will need to appreciate that the library website is more complex than those of other departments.

The academic library Director will not make the website and related applications, but how they look and work will reflect back on the Director. The political role of the Director is to build a research-based consensus among library staff about the characteristics of effective academic websites, social media, and mobile applications, and then share that with web staff across campus. Non-library web staff may have limited experience with academic library websites, the library user interface research, or the messaging and sharing roles of social media in libraries. The intent is to influence the look of the library website, social media, and mobile applications and the ease of their use.

Professional Development

There is considerable research on what works best for students when using an academic library website. It is wise to promote professional development for all library staff on the topic of what makes an exemplary academic library website. The intent is to move the staff past their own likes and dislikes, and move toward some research-based guidelines on usability. The staff in the campus departments who actually make and maintain the library website may not know much about library websites and the usability research. One role is to help them transfer this research and these models into practice for the library's website.

Web Analytics

If students and faculty use the library website, then for what and how often? When the website is developed, it is good to be aware of how its use can be monitored. Are there some parts of the site considered more important, and is there a way to determine the amount of traffic to those pages or links? There are a number of web analytics tools and resources. Ongoing evaluation needs to be part of the design.

Mobile

Faculty and students want web-based library content and the ability to comment, share, and receive notices. They want to do this not only through their desktop and laptop computers, but also through their smartphones and tablets. An academic library administrator and staff directly responsible for web-based content must make sure that the library's content, and the ability to comment and share, works equally well on mobile devices.

APPLICATION

Institutional Home Page

The word "library" must appear on the institutional home page, or else the library "doesn't exist" for faculty and students. If the word "library" doesn't appear, then someone who wants to use the library has to first search for the library home page. There is a lot of money involved in operating the library, and it seems odd to hide the library home page, or in some way require multiple steps to find it. The academic library Director needs to use some political skill with whomever controls the institution's website in order for the word "library" to be obvious on its home page. This is not an option.

Usability Research

An academic library administrator should have a high-level understanding of academic website usability research, and set the conditions for staff professional development on this topic. It is helpful to bring the whole library staff into this question and do a workshop, asking "What makes for valid usability testing, and what has been learned?" Exploring with the whole staff the process and results of usability testing is the best way to get most staff beyond "my whims and your whims." Patrons come to a library website looking for specific information, and the goal of good design (and, hence, usability testing) is to provide the right visual clues, and get the user to the desired content with the fewest clicks. In addition to staff professional development, web design and usability testing might be a good collaborative project between library staff and a faculty member with a class interested in a project.

Style Manual

The quality of the writing on an academic library website either generates in its readers a sense of trust in this library, or raises a series of concerns about the overall quality of the information and work done by this library staff. Academic faculty particularly notice indifferent and inconsistent writing, which leaves an impression of the library as below standard. One good way to sustain confidence among users of the library website is to develop a library style manual and use it on library website pages, and on all internally written documents linked to the website. Correct grammar, punctuation, spelling, and syntax, along with internal consistency in terminology, will give the impression that the people at this library know how to write and operate at a level expected in an academic institution.

Automated Messages

Many automated messages about library business go to patrons via e-mail. An administrator should have somebody look at all of these and consider if they are clear, and if they portray the library's image in the right way. They need to be checked against the library's "Style Manual." It is common to have a variety of automated messages written over the years by various people or companies. Some messages come bundled with a vendor's software, and can't be changed. Of messages which staff can control, it is good to look at all of them as a group, and ask if the wording projects the image and tone desired from the library.

Staff Directory

The library website needs an easy-to-find library staff directory. Students and faculty often need to know whom to contact. Useful staff directories have photographs taken with the same background, and presented in a way that makes the library staff look like the professionals they are.

READING

STANDARDS AND GUIDELINES

Association of College and Research Libraries. "Standards for Libraries in Higher Education." Chicago: American Library Association, 2011. www.ala.org/acrl/standards/standardslibraries.

ADVICE AND RESEARCH

Fagan, Jody Condit, and Jennifer A. Keach. *Web Project Management for Academic Libraries*. Oxford: Chandos Publishing, 2009.

Journal of Web Librarianship. www.lib.jmu.edu/org/jwl.

King, David Lee. *Face2Face: Using Facebook, Twitter, and Other Social Media Tools to Create Great Customer Connections*. Medford, NJ: Information Today, Inc., 2012.

Krug, Steve. Advanced Common Sense. www.sensible.com.

Krug, Steve. *Don't Make Me Think: A Common Sense Approach to Web Usability*, 2nd ed. Berkeley, CA: New Riders, 2006.

Krug, Steve. *Rocket Surgery Made Easy: The Do-It-Yourself Guide to Finding and Fixing Usability Problems*. Berkeley, CA: New Riders, 2010.

Lehman, Tom, and Terry Nikkel, eds. *Making Library Web Sites Usable: A LITA Guide*. New York: Neal-Schuman Publishers, Inc., 2008.

Marek, Kate. "Using Web Analytics in the Library." *Library Technology Reports* 47, no. 5. Chicago: American Library Association, 2011.

Nielsen, Jakob. Nielson Norman Group. www.useit.com.

Prasse, Michael J., and Lynn Silipigni Connaway. "Usability Testing: Method and Research." In *Academic Library Research: Perspectives and Current Trends,* edited by Marie L. Radford and Pamela Snelson. Chicago: Association of College and Research Libraries, 2008.

Reeb, Brenda. *Design Talk: Understanding the Roles of Usability Practitioners, Web Designers, and Web Developers in User-Centered Web Design.* Chicago: Association of College and Research Libraries, 2008.

Singley, Emily. "Usable Libraries." http://emilysingley.net.

Singley, Emily. "Top 10 Academic Library Websites 2012." Usable Libraries. http://emilysingley.net/top-10-academic-library-websites-2012.

Steiner, Sarah K. *Strategic Planning for Social Media in Libraries.* Chicago: American Library Association, 2012.

27
Technology

As Good As Anywhere on Campus

ASSERTION

The academic library Director is responsible for the library's electronic infrastructure, computers, software, mobile devices, peripheral equipment, and the use of such by library staff being as good as that found any other place on campus.

COMMENTARY

Working Relationship

The working relationship between the relevant staff in the library and the Information Technology department is of the highest importance, because the library is dependent upon the Information Technology department, and the library is an important user of services provided by Information Technology. The academic library Director and leader of Information Technology set the context for mutual respect among employees from each group. These employees need to work well together in order to obtain and maintain the library technology. If there isn't an effective, sustained working relationship, and if all parts of the campus and library technology do not work well together (e.g., wired and wireless network, computers, software, authentication, and training), then students and faculty will drift away from using electronic content through the library. The usefulness and status of the library are tied directly to the quality of services provided by the Information Technology department. The political fortunes of each are intertwined. While they may have different reporting relationships, they need to work together.

Electronic Infrastructure

The library Director needs to understand at a basic level the campus network infrastructure, the network connection to the library, and the infrastructure within the building (e.g., wiring closets, network wiring in the ceiling and walls, the building's wireless points, and how the security system works). The purpose is both to know how all aspects of the campus system work, but also to support the Information Technology requests for upgrades to any part of the campus network. The library needs to be a political supporter of the Information Technology efforts. Being a supporter gets the library a seat at the table, and some influence over decisions ranging from buying infrastructure components, equipping classrooms, and choosing computer hardware and peripherals, to training and policy questions on usage.

Early Adopters

The Director should encourage some staff to be "early adopters" and use new devices, software programs, and social media. Academic library blogs are full of references to librarians who find ways to use new technology in librarianship. The Director needs to have a discretionary fund and space for staff to buy and try new technology, including off-line. An attitude of experimentation with new technology within the library is good for the early adopters who thrive on new innovation, and it is good over time for the library. This is another example where a dotted-line relationship is important between the right people in the library and those in the Information Technology department. It is also an example of how library staff need to be innovators on campus with the use of new technology. Mastering, using, and teaching about existing technology should be a given, but so is the need for some library staff to be leaders in the acquisition and use of new consumer technology.

Operating Systems

Does it matter what kind of computers (and computing devices) the library provides for staff and patron use? The answer is that what is used by the

Director, staff, and supplied for patron use all need to be whatever the Information Technology department buys and supports. If the Information Technology policy is to buy and support several brands of devices and several operating systems, then it is fine for library staff to use multiple devices and operating systems. But if the Information Technology department buys and supports one brand of devices and one operating system, then the Director needs to be clear: while at work all staff need to use the machine and operating system the institution issues and supports. The Director does not want to get the library in the position of being perceived as a renegade by the Information Technology department. There are better ways of moving to "both/and" other than buying for staff non-supported devices and operating systems, just because some individuals like one brand or operating system more than the one supported by the institution.

Enterprise Software

Whatever enterprise software is provided by the institution is what library staff must use. This especially refers to e-mail, word processing, and calendar software. While it is unlikely that staff would want to use other products (or in some cases be able to), this is another example of where it is better to use what is provided for everyone in the institution, and not be an outlier.

Duplication

The library staff should let the Information Technology group do those tasks which it is currently doing for the rest of the campus (e.g., the act of evaluating, buying, installing, maintaining, and disposing of computers, operating the wired and wireless network, installing enterprise software, and making decisions about the networked print, copy, and scan devices). Tasks that are best done by the Information Technology and other departments on campus should be done by those departments, and not duplicated by library staff. Library staff should work on tasks that really are unique to the library, and what other campus departments aren't doing.

APPLICATION

Equipment

Most students bring laptops, tablets, or smartphones into the library, and use the library's wireless network. What kind of access equipment should the library provide without duplicating what students and faculty already own (and would probably prefer to use)? The number of installed desktop computers for public use should be evaluated periodically, and perhaps reduced. This is related to the number of computers needed during peak usage times, and the reallocation of funds within the library budget. In addition to desktop computers, what other kinds of equipment should the library provide? It should provide:

- higher-end computers,
- computers at movable tables with plenty of room to work,
- two screens at computers located where students are likely to research and write,
- screens on a movable arm so that the angle and height can be adjusted,
- software that students likely don't have,
- large screens for group work, especially in small-group workrooms,
- scanning equipment, especially for book pages, and
- printing, including in color and poster size.

Studio/Workshop Space

As part of the library's educational role with students, the librarians teach how to find and use information. The "use information" part means that the library needs a staffed space where students may receive help with the technology they use to produce evidence of their learning, such as editing video or sound, making presentations, using spreadsheets, analyzing data, or printing posters. A studio/workshop area can often be made by repurposing underused space (such as space used to store back runs of paper journals on open shelving). It can be staffed with student workers, trained in use of the applications available in the studio/workshop. The library should provide training, equipment, and studio/workshop space for students who want to use various technology tools and applications as part of their learning.

Library Software Spreadsheet

The library is dependent upon a variety of software and externally hosted systems running on the campus network. It is very helpful to define all of these on a spreadsheet, with the current version and date, and keep this spreadsheet on an intranet site where library and Information Technology staff can see it. Additionally, this spreadsheet needs to list the person on the library staff who is the primary contact for this application. This level of communication builds working relationships between library and Information Technology staff, and leads to inclusion when making decisions about changing anything on this spreadsheet. There are so many technical details that can conflict and disrupt service; a comprehensive spreadsheet should help with uneventful operations.

Staff Understanding and Use of Technology

It is not just the academic library Director and one or several library technology staff who need to understand how the campus and library electronic infrastructure works, and how to use various software and applications. Library staff interact with patrons to help them with technology issues, or explain why they can't do something. Hence, it is smart to have someone who works with technology, either from the library staff or Information Technology, teach the whole library staff how the campus network works, how the networks and enterprise software work within the library, and why certain parts need to be upgraded. Additionally, staff meetings or retreats should have a technology component, ranging from "here is how the system works" to "here is how you use this piece of software."

Servers

Owning, maintaining, and using computer servers in the library should be rare. Servers should be owned and managed by the campus Information Technology department or cloud-based vendors or organizations. This has implications for leasing space instead of purchasing servers, and not having to allocate FTE for server maintenance and backup. If the campus connection to the library is sufficiently robust, then the need for actual server boxes in the library is minimal.

READING

STANDARDS AND GUIDELINES

Association of College and Research Libraries. "Standards for Libraries in Higher Education." Chicago: American Library Association, 2011. www.ala.org/acrl/standards/standardslibraries.

ADVICE AND RESEARCH

ACRL Research Planning and Review Committee. "Environmental Scan 2013." Chicago: Association of College and Research Libraries, 2013. www.ala.org/acrl/sites/ala.org.acrl/files/content/publications/whitepapers/EnvironmentalScan13.pdf.

ALA TechSource. www.alatechsource.org.

Alire, Camila A., and G. Edward Evans. *Academic Librarianship.* New York: Neal-Schuman Publishers, Inc., 2010.

Council on Library and Information Resources. www.clir.org.

Greene, Courtney, Roser, Missy, and Ruane, Elizabeth. *The Anywhere Library: A Primer for the Mobile Web.* Chicago: Association of College and Research Libraries, 2010.

Groves, Christy, and Heather Lambert. "The Library As Partner: Sustaining Relevance in a Collaborative, Student-Focused Technology Center." In *The Entrepreneurial Librarian: Essays on the Infusion of Private-Business Dynamism into the Professional Service,* edited by Mary Krautter, Mary Beth Lock, and Mary G. Scanlon. Jefferson, NC: McFarland & Company, Inc., Publishers, 2012.

Iglesias, Edward, ed. *An Overview of the Changing Role of the Systems Librarian: Systemic Shifts.* Oxford: Chandos Publishing, 2010.

Knox, Karen C. *Implementing Technology Solutions in Libraries: Techniques, Tools, and Tips From the Trenches.* Medford, NJ: Information Today, Inc., 2011.

Mash, S. David. *Decision-Making in the Absence of Certainty: A Study in the Context of Technology and the Construction of the 21st Century Academic Library.* Chicago: American Library Association, 2011.

Mates, Barbara T. *Assistive Technologies in the Library.* Chicago: American Library Association, 2011.

28
Open Access to Information

Evidence of High Value

ASSERTION

The academic library Director sets the context so that data ranging from information about the library to open-access journals and data curation services all demonstrate the high value placed on open access to information.

COMMENTARY

Open Access

Academic library administrators and librarians ought to support efforts which promote or provide open access to information, and especially open access to articles, journals, theses, dissertations, images, and digitized books. Open-access journals, repositories, and search engines provide some free and open access to scholarly articles, even though access to much of this literature in more prestigious journals is controlled by commercial vendors. Libraries will continue to distinguish between peer-reviewed articles and those without some level of vetting, whether obtained commercially or through open access.

A high percentage of libraries in institutions where teaching has higher value than research are effectively priced out of licensing some journals at various levels of prestige, or even licensing very many journals at all. Access is driven by the library's ability to pay, and student or faculty members having access to such libraries. The move toward some open-access scholarly information has implications for an academic library, especially if articles can be accessed by anyone on the Internet. The library then becomes one of several silos competing for faculty and student attention. An academic library offers vetted sources on the Internet, whether commercially licensed or through an open-access source. Open-access initiatives will continue to emerge and, depending on the size and purpose of the library, an academic library Director needs to keep current with open-access developments and their practical impact on the daily operation of a library.

Scholarly Communication

Scholarly communication refers to ways of making scholarly work available outside of traditional publishing of books and journal articles, usually through free and open online digital repositories, created and hosted by academic libraries. The library's role in scholarly communications begins with faculty and student desires for digital space to safely house and share their work, and access the work of others stored in similar repositories. On campuses where digital forms of scholarly communication are of interest, then library staff would likely play a leading role in defining and managing scholarly communication efforts, although in conjunction with other campus units. Issues of copyright and sharing have changed with the Creative Commons (CC) licenses.

Data Curation

Some faculty and students have data they have generated for a project, whether original or obtained from other sources. They not only want to store it safely, but are open to sharing it, and also letting others use it for other projects, which may add value to it. Data could be in the form of a spreadsheet, social science research, or scientific research results. Especially in research-oriented universities, librarians can provide advice and guidelines during the research process that will make it feasible to keep the data, deliver ongoing technical help about storing various iterations, provide storage space, and make it possible for others to retrieve it.

Write It

For accreditation, for good customer service, and because this is what well-run organizations do, the Director must see that all library policies and procedures are written down and made available on the library website. Anyone in the campus community should be able to easily find library policies and procedures through the site. Who approved a policy and when it was approved should be on the document. While it may not be accessed very often, it is nevertheless helpful to be clear about the use of the library and its resources.

Transparency

The reason for writing down library policies and procedures and making them easily accessible on the library website is transparency for patrons regarding basic information about the library. Library patrons should not be surprised by any library policy or procedure. Neither library staff nor patrons should say "We didn't know" or "We can't remember" or "The person I asked gave the wrong answer." Write it down, and make it easy to find on the website. That sends a clear message that this library values correct information, that someone monitors the currency of information on this website, and that anyone in the campus community can see these internal policies and procedures.

APPLICATION
Basic Information About the Library

Patrons go to the library website expecting to find certain kinds of information about the library. Academic library administrators and staff should agree on the basic information that should be on the website. It most likely will include:

- days and hours the library is open,
- names, titles, photographs, and contact information for all staff,
- definition of who may access or borrow each type of library material,
- information about the loan periods for each type of patron, each type of material, and the fine schedule,
- Annual Reports of the library, and
- definition of who may reserve and use library spaces, and how to do that.

READING

STANDARDS AND GUIDELINES

Association of College and Research Libraries. "Standards for Libraries in Higher Education." Chicago: American Library Association, 2011. www.ala.org/acrl/standards/standardslibraries.

Association of College and Research Libraries. "Scholarly Communication." Chicago: Association of College and Research Libraries. www.ala.org/acrl/issues/scholcomm.

Association of College and Research Libraries. "Scholarly Communication Toolkit." Chicago: Association of College and Research Libraries. http://scholcomm.acrl.ala.org.

ADVICE AND RESEARCH

Association of College and Research Libraries. *Intersections of Scholarly Communication and Information Literacy: Creating Strategic Collaborations for a Changing Academic Environment.* Chicago: Association of College and Research Libraries, 2013. http://acrl.ala.org/intersections.

Bailey, Charles W., Jr., *Digital Curation Bibliography: Preservation and Stewardship of Scholarly Works.* Houston, TX: Digital Scholarship, 2012. http://digital-scholarship.org/dcbw/dcb.pdf.

Bailey, Charles W. Jr., "What Is Open Access?" In *Open Access: Key Strategic, Technical and Economic Aspects*, edited by Neil Jacobs. Oxford: Chandos Publishing, 2006.

Burgett, Shelly Wood. "If It Isn't Written, It Doesn't Exist: Creating a Library Policy Manual." In *It's All About Student Learning. Managing Community and Other College Libraries in the 21st Century*, edited by David R. Dowell and Gerard B. McCabe. Westport, CT: Libraries Unlimited, 2006.

Crawford, Walt. *Open Access. What You Need to Know Now.* Chicago: American Librarian Association, 2011.

"Creative Commons." http://creativecommons.org.

"Data Curation." Council on Library and Information Resources. www.clir.org/initiatives-partnerships/data-curation.

"DH Curation Guide: A Community Resource Guide to Data Curation in the Digital Humanities." http://guide.dhcuration.org/index.html.

Harvey, Ross. *Digital Curation: A How-to-Do-It Manual.* New York: Neal-Schuman Publishers, 2010.

Mullen, Laura Bowering. *Open Access and Its Practical Impact on the Work of Academic Librarians: Collection Development, Public Services, and the Library and Information Science Literature.* Oxford: Chandos Publishing, 2010.

"SPARC, the Scholarly Publishing & Academic Resources Coalition." www.arl.org/sparc/index.shtml.

Swan, Alma. "Overview of Scholarly Communication." In *Open Access: Key Strategic, Technical and Economic Aspects,* edited by Neil Jacobs. Oxford: Chandos Publishing, 2006.

Tenopir, Carol, Ben Birch, and Suzie Allard. "Academic Libraries and Research Data Services: Current Practices and Plans for the Future. An ACRL White Paper." Association of College and Research Libraries, 2012. www.ala.org/acrl/sites/ala.org.acrl/files/content/publications/whitepapers/Tenopir_Birch_Allard.pdf.

Willinsky, John. *The Access Principle: The Case for Open Access to Research and Scholarship.* Cambridge, MA: The MIT Press, 2006.

29
Intellectual Property

Define, Educate, and Model

ASSERTION

An academic library administrator helps lead an ongoing campus effort to define ethical creation, use, and sharing of intellectual property, and implements ways to educate about and model the use of those definitions.

COMMENTARY

Intellectual Property

Academic library administrators should provide (or share in providing) leadership for a campus effort to establish (and maintain) guidelines about the creation, use, and dissemination of intellectual property. One aspect is the ongoing understanding of what copyright means in specific practice. Another part is scholarly communication, which deals with ownership and access of faculty and student work outside of traditional publication. There is considerable material written on both topics. The institution needs policies and procedures in place regarding the ownership and use of intellectual property. Library administrators should play a leading role in that effort for their institutions, both in definition, implementation, and ongoing revision.

Authoritative Websites

A basic role the library can play regarding copyright is to provide links from the library website to the most authoritative websites that have guidelines and answers to copyright questions. Librarians and frontline staff will receive copyright questions, and they need to know how to answer questions of copyright, or the sources to which questioners can be referred. Being clear on the answers to copyright questions (or where those answers can be found) is a good staff development topic.

Working with Other Departments

There are several campus groups with an interest in copyright in addition to the library. The Information Technology department plays a role with student use of content on the institution's network; specifically, downloading and sharing movies, images, and music. The Print department is interested in copyright compliance for reproduction of printed material. The library is interested in the use of a wide variety of physical and virtual content. Faculty are interested in curbing student plagiarism. Academic departments may be interested in scholarly communication efforts. Attorneys for the institution need to pay attention to all of this. An ideal approach is for several groups to work together and write one statement for use in the institution, and make that statement available on multiple websites and pages.

Scholarly Communications

In institutions where faculty and graduate students research, write, and publish, and depending on the library's budget, personnel, and consortial connections, librarians could assist graduate students and faculty by providing:

- Institutional Repository space,
- advice on options for publishing and disseminating written work,
- referral services to open-access journals and sites, or
- hosting an open-access journal and sites.

What that means in practice depends on the type of institution, and the recent experience of faculty and students looking to librarians for these services.

APPLICATION

Students

Learning about the ethical use of information is not a priority for many students. Librarians need to find clever ways to teach about information ethics, without driving away students. Some librarians have made or used witty videos on copyright applications.

Modeling Copyright Compliance

Library staff need to model compliance with copyright procedures when using content. That means noting permission when they use copyrighted material in their teaching. It also means written clarity with faculty about reserves, copying, and material posted on course management sites.

Questions to Staff

Faculty and students will likely ask anyone who works in the library for an opinion about the use of copyrighted material. It is wise to have the word "copyright" in a visible place on the library website, linking to a page of copyright questions and answers. Indeed, other campus groups should link to this same page. Librarians and staff need to be part of a coordinated campus effort to define and then disseminate what is acceptable use of intellectual property. All library staff should know about this copyright page, the answers to most questions, and what to say if there isn't an answer. That may require a consensus that knowledge about copyright practices is a good use of time, and then an ongoing investment in different levels of professional development.

Creative Commons

Librarians should know about Creative Commons (CC) licenses (http://creativecommons.org), and guide faculty and students to that website for potential use with digital work. Using a CC license is a good way to protect intellectual property on the Internet which the author wants to share, or to legally use Internet material for which the originator gives permission.

READING

STANDARDS AND GUIDELINES

Association of College and Research Libraries. "Scholarly Communication." Chicago: Association of College and Research Libraries. www.ala.org/acrl/issues/scholcomm.

Association of College and Research Libraries. "Scholarly Communication Toolkit."
    Chicago: Association of College and Research Libraries. http://scholcomm.acrl
    .ala.org.

Association of College and Research Libraries. "Standards for Libraries in Higher
    Education." Chicago: American Library Association, 2011. www.ala.org/acrl/
    standards/standardslibraries.

Association of College and Research Libraries. "Statement on Fair Use and Electronic
    Reserves." Chicago: Association of College and Research Libraries, 2003.
    www.ala.org/acrl/publications/whitepapers/statementfair.

ADVICE AND RESEARCH

ACRL Research Planning and Review Committee. "Environmental Scan 2013."
    Chicago: Association of College and Research Libraries, 2013. www.ala
    .org/acrl/sites/ala.org.acrl/files/content/publications/whitepapers/
    EnvironmentalScan13.pdf.

Alire, Camila A., and G. Edward Evans. *Academic Librarianship*. New York: Neal-
    Schuman Publishers, Inc., 2010.

Bailey, Charles W. Jr., "What Is Open Access?" In *Open Access: Key Strategic, Technical
    and Economic Aspects*, edited by Neil Jacobs. Oxford: Chandos Publishing, 2006.

Budd, John M. *The Changing Academic Library: Operations, Culture, Environments*. 2nd
    ed. Chicago: Association of College and Research Libraries, 2012.

Cornell Copyright Information Center. http://copyright.cornell.edu.

Creative Commons. http://creativecommons.org.

Crews, Kenneth. Copyright Advisory Office. Columbia University Libraries/
    Information Services. http://copyright.columbia.edu/copyright.

Crews, Kenneth D. *Copyright Law for Librarians and Educators: Creative Strategies and
    Practical Solutions,* 3rd Edition. Chicago: American Library Association, 2012.

Hirtle, Peter B. "Copyright Term and the Public Domain in the United States." Cornell
    Copyright Information Center, January 2012. http://copyright.cornell.edu/
    resources/publicdomain.cfm.

Mullen, Laura Bowering. *Open Access and Its Practical Impact on the Work of Academic
    Librarians: Collection Development, Public Services, and the Library and Information
    Science Literature*. Oxford: Chandos Publishing, 2010.

Peters, Timothy. "Copyright to the University: Tips on Informing, Educating, and
    Enabling." *College & Research Libraries News* 72, no. 10 (November 2011).

Swan, Alma. "Overview of Scholarly Communication." In *Open Access: Key Strategic, Technical and Economic Aspects*, edited by Neil Jacobs. Oxford: Chandos Publishing, 2006.

"UW Copyright Connection." Seattle: University of Washington. http://depts .washington.edu/uwcopy.

University of Washington Libraries. "Copyright Information for Educators." www.lib .washington.edu/help/guides/copyright.html.

30
Assessment

Describe, Understand, and Use

ASSERTION

The academic library Director establishes and budgets for a data-collection effort through which staff can describe and understand the library's part of the overall educational program, and use some of this data in decision-making.

COMMENTARY

Assessment

It is easy to not collect, or to collect and ignore, data about library performance. Library staff are busy doing their jobs. Collecting, interpreting, and using data so often seems like an "add on." Nevertheless, people in many sectors collect, interpret, and use data to understand how they are doing, how their work contributes to the overall work of the institution, where they need to change, and what they need to do better. That is what the academic library Director and staff also need to do.

The Director needs to establish and sustain a culture among the library staff where the collection and use of some data are a normal part of operating the library. The cost of doing this is time, budget, and overcoming the perceived low value of the data. The faculty and students are the "customers" of the library. If the library staff have a customer-driven orientation, then library leadership needs to know what aspects of the library are being used, and what the customers wish the library provided. Librarians need to understand the usefulness of their instruction, and how it is part of learning outcomes. To do these means working with individuals in the institution who collect and analyze data, and deciding what library data fits with overall institutional data collection. The administrative task is to build a culture that collects and uses data, which becomes one factor in helping understand how to change aspects of the library so that it is part of the institution's educational mix.

Systematic Collection of Data

The collection of data about the library is driven by:

- an internal need-to-know,
- the need-to-show library success to institutional leaders, and
- the accreditation process.

The need-to-know means watching indicators of usage of the building, staff time, library resources, and their impact on learning. Tracking the same data and posting it show early indicators of changes. Sharing parts of this data with campus leaders and the faculty can show how the library is integrated into teaching, learning outcomes, and research. Accreditation is a compelling external reason to assess aspects of the library program, staff, budget, intellectual content, technology, and the building, and then try to develop plausible responses. Whether need-to-know, need-to-show, or accreditation, the hard part is to correctly interpret cause and effect. The challenge is to understand what some data mean in context. All of that begins with systematic collection of data.

Using Data

The Director needs to help library staff and campus administrators understand what the data means about the library. The challenge is to know what data to watch, what it means in context, and if indeed the data is sufficiently valid and meaningful to require a change (and what that change might cost in terms of budget and political capital). It is hard to show cause and effect, as there are clearly factors out of the control of library staff, and these factors can alter the data.

It is also hard to determine realistic standards against which library performance should be judged. The task is to "benchmark" a library's data against comparable data that is judged to be a desirable standard. Performance data needs to be compared to:

- expectations within this institution for library services,
- available budget,
- data from comparable libraries, and
- external benchmarks.

In using data to conclude something about the level of quality for a library, the administrative challenge is to judge if staff and user expectations are too low, or too high and beyond what can be delivered. It is very hard to raise low expectations. It is equally hard to keep expecting staff to deliver content and services when the library doesn't have the budget to buy that content (leading to frustration and apologizing), or an adequate number of staff for expected services (leading to sour attitudes, health problems, and resignations). The Director needs to be blunt about the expected levels of library services (which are driven by a realistic understanding of the budget), and how to talk to patrons about what the library can and cannot provide.

Building and Materials Usage

The count of people entering the library, and the indicators showing the use of physical and electronic materials, are coarse indicators of library usage. They don't tell much that is useful about who enters the library, when, and for what purposes, or who is using books, e-journals, and databases. However, these indicators are noticed by other administrators, especially when mulling campus-wide questions of budget and facilities. It is important to keep numbers for the gate count, item checkout, and use of electronic resources all within an acceptable range. Keeping the gate count number as high as possible matters, even if that means a variety of uses that expand traditional uses of the library building. When building and materials usage numbers move up or down from levels of previous years, then the Director and staff need to ask why, hopefully understand cause and effect correctly, and take corrective action if possible.

Accreditation

The library Director needs to take the accreditation process seriously, both because of the political consequences (positive and negative) for the library and the institution, but also because the accreditation process:

- helps library staff benchmark the library performance against external standards,
- requires the library staff to write or revise all foundational documents,
- means that someone who is an outsider (but who knows about libraries) is going to look at your library, and
- can be a useful external event for the Director to "blame" during the process of making desired internal changes.

Almost all libraries will meet the minimal accreditation standards. An accreditation self-study is helpful when the process makes evident areas for improvement, and then the administrators and staff work on that.

Accreditation Strategy

The library may well rise or fall politically within the institution depending on the results of the accreditation process. It is in the best interests of the library if the Director understands the accreditation questions, collects the right data annually, and uses that data in an ongoing way to answer the accreditation questions. A commendation can be of significant help in sustaining or raising the status of the library among top administrators. It is rarely in the self-interest of the library when the accreditation report singles out the library for deficiencies. That is usually understood as external affirmation of what is already known by institutional decision-makers.

Secondary Accreditation

Many graduate programs are accredited by a national professional association. The library is one part of this "secondary accreditation" review. Consequently, the librarian responsible for library services to that discipline needs to know the expectations from this professional group, especially for specific library content. These professional accreditation reviews may expect to see different data or resources than the regional accreditation reviews of the institution. It is necessary to understand the expectations of both and collect data accordingly.

Comparative Statistics

There are several national surveys of academic libraries, and perhaps a regional survey. An academic library administrator needs to understand what each question is asking (each survey has definitions), and what that means for setting up daily internal processes to collect data the way each survey expects. If data is collected and reported in ways consistent with other libraries, then the survey results may be of use. Comparing one library against large norms doesn't usually tell much. It is more effective to make a spreadsheet of peer or aspirational schools. This spreadsheet may show which schools to investigate in order to learn what they do that could be replicated.

APPLICATION

Indicators

Evidence for the Annual Report, and hence the accreditation report, should come from traditional input and usage statistics. If part of a consortium, then borrowing statistics of physical items needs to show this consortial approach. Electronic usage is harder to show in meaningful ways. It is easier to ask good questions about who is using electronic resources and for what purposes than it is to show this. Project COUNTER (Counting Online Usage of NeTworked Electronic Resources) shows the complexity. It is very hard to show cause and effect, but there are some indicators which can show correlation. For example, the LibQUAL+ survey is helpful, but sometimes it is still hard to understand what students and faculty really meant and want when they filled out LibQUAL+. A focus group can be helpful. Another source of local evidence might come from institutional reviews of departments or programs if several library questions are built into these reviews. Accumulated class evaluations can show trends. A yearly conversation between a liaison librarian and faculty of a department can be helpful. Other indicators can come from ethnographic research, which usually means counting in-building usage and looking for other characteristics.

Annual Reports

The academic library Director needs to write an Annual Report of the library activities, complete with as much data as possible, showing what transpired in the library and comparing that data to previous years. The format should be similar to what is needed for accreditation purposes. These Annual Reports should roll up into the accreditation report. The data should be available on a library intranet, and the Annual Reports should also be easily accessible on the library website.

Accreditation Evaluator

The Director should volunteer to work at some level on the campus committee that provides oversight to the accreditation process. That is a good way to understand the questions, the institutional response, and how to position the library. The Director should also volunteer to the regional accrediting agency to be part of site visits that evaluate other schools. Being an evaluator of other libraries is a very helpful way to think about assessment of your library.

Sharing Statistics

What should the Director do with comparative statistics, and especially with a spreadsheet comparing statistics from similar schools? It can be politically awkward to promote these numbers if they are too good. Or, if the numbers are disappointing, they can harm the library's image, and indeed library staff morale. Evidence of weakness doesn't usually get rewarded in academic politics. Resources usually follow vision, not indicators of poor funding or performance. However, there are times when top administrators have increased library funding because it slipped below comparable schools. It takes some political skill to know what comparative data to share with whom, when, and for what intended purpose.

Assessing Instruction

There are multiple unobtrusive ways to collect data about the effectiveness of library instruction, and to incorporate that with other data about individual students, groups in academic majors, and performance compared to learning outcomes. The design of library assessment should be done in conjunction with institutional staff who collect and interpret data about students. The administrative task is to sustain a culture within the library where it is normal to collect data, and where that is done in conjunction with others on campus who are also interested in academic effectiveness. Having data showing the effectiveness of teaching will increase the visibility and status of librarians as players in the institution's educational efforts.

READING

STANDARDS AND GUIDELINES

Association of College and Research Libraries. "Standards for Libraries in Higher Education." Chicago: American Library Association, 2011. www.ala.org/acrl/standards/standardslibraries.

COUNTER. Counting Online Usage of NeTworked Electronic Resources. www.projectcounter.org.

ADVICE AND RESEARCH

Alire, Camila A., and G. Edward Evans. *Academic Librarianship*. New York: Neal-Schuman Publishers, Inc., 2010.

Budd, John M. *The Changing Academic Library: Operations, Culture, Environments*, 2nd ed. Chicago: Association of College and Research Libraries, 2012.

LibQUAL+. www.libqual.org/home.

Matthews, Joseph R. *Library Assessment in Higher Education*. Westport, CT: Libraries Unlimited, 2007.

Nelson, William Neal, and Robert W. Fernekes. *Standards and Assessment for Academic Libraries: A Workbook*. Chicago: Association of College and Research Libraries, 2002.

Radcliff, Carolyn J., Mary Lee Jensen, Joseph A. Salem, Jr., Kenneth J. Burhanna, and Julie A. Gedeon. *A Practical Guide to Information Literacy Assessment for Academic Librarians*. Westport, CT: Libraries Unlimited, 2007.

St. Clair, Gloriana. "Benchmarking and Restructuring." In *Restructuring Academic Libraries: Organizational Development in the Wake of Technological Change, Publications in Librarianship No. 49*. Chicago: Association of College and Research Libraries. www.ala.org/acrl/publications/booksanddigitalresources/booksmonographs/pil/pil49/pil49restructuring.

Wood, Elizabeth J., Rush Miller, and Amy Knapp. *Beyond Survival. Managing Academic Libraries in Transition*. Westport, CT: Libraries Unlimited, 2007.

Woodward, Jeannette. *Creating the Customer-Driven Academic Library*. Chicago: American Library Association, 2009.

Index